On Stage

200 Years of Great Theatrical Personalities

On Stage

Monroe H. Fabian

Foreword by Livingston L. Biddle, Jr.

A Main Street Press Book
Published by Mayflower Books, Inc., U.S.A. New York

Library of Congress Catalog Card Number 79-87676
ISBN 8317-6602-6

Published by Mayflower Books, Inc., U.S.A.
575 Lexington Avenue, New York City 10022

Produced by The Main Street Press, Inc.
William Case House
Pittstown, New Jersey 08867

Designed by Carl Berkowitz

Printed in the United States of America

In my study . . . I have often sat until dawn, alternately reading memoirs of the great actors of the past, and contemplating their portraits and death-masks which hang upon the walls; and somehow I seem to derive a more satisfactory idea of their capabilities from their counterfeit presentments than from the written records of their lives.

Edwin Booth, 1886

Contents

Foreword by Livingston L. Biddle, Jr. 9
Introduction 15

Nancy Hallam 26
George Frederick Cooke 28
John Durang 30
Edmund Kean 32
William B. Wood 38
William Charles Macready 40
Junius Brutus Booth 42
James Henry Hackett 44
Paul Taglioni and Amalia Taglioni 46
Mary Ann Wood 48
Edwin Forrest 52
Ira Aldridge 55
Fanny Kemble 58
Clara Fisher 60
Fanny Elssler 62
Charlotte Cushman 65
Jenny Lind 73
Dion Boucicault 76
Mary Ann Lee 78
Augusta Maywood 80
John McCullough 82
Joseph Jefferson 84
Edwin Booth 89
Richard Mansfield 94
Otis Skinner 96
Loïe Fuller 98
Julia Marlowe 102
Minnie Maddern Fiske 104
Carmencita 106
Maude Adams 108
Enrico Caruso 110
Feodor Chaliapin 114
Fritz Kreisler 116
Josef Hofmann 118
Ruth St. Denis and Ted Shawn 120
Isadora Duncan 124

Ethel Barrymore   127
Nazimova   130
Walter Hampden   132
John Barrymore   134
Pavlova   142
Geraldine Farrar   144
John McCormack   146
Howard Lindsay and Dorothy Stickney   148
Lauritz Melchior   150
Jeanne Eagels   152
Alfred Lunt and Lynn Fontanne   154
Mae West   156
Fay Bainter   158
Clifton Webb   160
Katharine Cornell   162
Paul Robeson   164
Gertrude Lawrence   167
Lotte Lenya   170
Helen Hayes   177
Martha Graham   180
Maurice Evans   182
Tallulah Bankhead   184
Gregor Piatigorsky   186
John Gielgud   188
Angna Enters   190
Lucia Chase   192
Benny Goodman   194
Ethel Merman   196
Alicia Markova   200
Zero Mostel   202
Lena Horne   204
Maria Callas   206
Regina Resnik   208
Marilyn Horne   211
Elvis Presley   214
Joan Baez   216
Jimi Hendrix   218

Credits   221
Index of Artists   223

Foreword

It has been almost 150 years since the introduction of the camera, and we of the late twentieth century have become fascinated by the multiple images that the various photographic processes can provide for us. We take for granted an ever-present abundance of images of both the famous and the infamous. Frequently, the painted and the modeled or sculpted image seems old-fashioned to many of us. Indeed, since the demands made today upon painters and sculptors are not as manifest as they were a century and a half ago for portraiture, it *is* the photographic image that often best conveys the features and the character of the individual involved. The multiplicity of photographs has served, however, to create an aura about the painted portrait or the piece of sculpture that makes it into something very special. As traditional or "old-fashioned" in concept as a likeness may be, such an image is frequently unique.

From the days of the painter Charles Willson Peale to the present, every generation of Americans has been able to see admirable works of art which have been based upon scenes from plays and opera or the dance, or which are depictions of the notable performing artists themselves. While the introduction of the camera served to provide us with volumes of photographic images of the great names of the stage, painters and sculptors have also been active in delineating excellence in performing areas, which enrich our lives and bring new insights to us all. And there is an amalgamation of painting and photography. More than a few painters and sculptors of both the nineteenth and twentieth centuries have utilized the camera in the process of creating a painting or a piece of sculpture.

With or without the camera to assist them, American artists left a colorful record of theatrical activity since the time shortly before the American Revolution. While depictions of theatrical activity that date from the eighteenth century are rare, from early in the nineteenth century we have been provided a visual feast of artwork inspired by the star performances of the leading personalities of the American stage. The types and styles of theater portraiture produced run the gamut from tobacco labels and cigar bands, garnished with tiny portraits of performers, to lithographed sheet music covers and chromolithographed posters, to "formal" depictions of actors, actresses, singers, and dancers posing in costume or shown just as they appeared on stage in the magic moments of those roles in which they made theatrical history.

Sculptors, too, have paid homage to the artists of the stage with their particular art. In a special manner, the sculptors provided aficionados with three-dimensional depictions of their favorite performers. While a few of the sculptures were full-sized and intended for public places, most were of small scale.

Except when included in thematic exhibitions or exhibitions featuring the work of artists with a particular interest in the theater, the full range of American artwork based upon the performing arts has not been adequately examined. While a book such as this is admittedly only prologue to the work that could be accomplished dealing with the subject matter of the fine and decorative arts inspired by the performing arts, it is a highly engaging beginning.

Monroe H. Fabian has been a member of the research and curatorial staff of the National Portrait Gallery, Smithsonian Institution, since 1966. He has also, since his teens, had a keen interest in the performing arts. In 1971, after two years of research, he orchestrated for the National Portrait Gallery the exhibition *Portraits of the American Stage: 1771-1971*, as a salute to the opening of The John F. Kennedy Center for the Performing Arts. Featuring painting, sculpture, costumes, theatrical memorabilia, and a continuous tape of the sounds of great stage performances, the installation was one of the most popular ever presented at the National Portrait Gallery. The exhibition demonstrated that a visual history lesson could be both instructive and entertaining. Built upon the now-out-of-print catalogue of the exhibition, this present volume combines serious scholarship with glimpses into personalities to provide an entertaining introduction to the study of the iconography of the performing arts.

Livingston L. Biddle, Jr.
Chairman
National Endowment for the Arts

On Stage

Introduction

Writing in 1886, the prince of American actors, Edwin Booth, noted that the "counterfeit presentments" of earlier thespians which he had in his personal collection told him more of their acting capabilities than written records. He was correct. A good picture or a detailed sculpture by an observant and talented artist is almost always more evocative than the proverbial thousand words written by a theater critic.

While theatrical presentation in what is now the United States may have begun as early as 1665, it was not until the third quarter of the eighteenth century that the appearance of any of its actors and actresses was recorded for us. The earliest known portrait of an identifiable person from the American stage is Charles Willson Peale's lovely painting of Nancy Hallam, first exhibited in Annapolis, Maryland, in September of 1771 (p. 33). It is indeed the cornerstone of American art of the theater.

For convenience, and to satisfy those who insist upon orderly categories as a means of understanding art, we can talk of four specific types of portraits of the performing arts.

The first type is the portrait of an actor, actress, or musician in what we might call civilian dress. Much of the portraiture of performing artists gives no hint of their profession. These are most certainly not the pictures that inspired Edwin Booth in his midnight musings. Within the sartorial tastes of each of the sitter's times, these portraits show the actor or actress posing merely in Sunday best or, in more recent times, in casual attire. Except for a certain perceptible air of self-confidence, many of the performers cannot be easily distinguished from the merchants, tradesmen, and educators who posed for the same artists. Occasionally, however, that certain air of self-confidence speaks more of the theatricality of the sitter and the sitter's profession than any stage costume could. Irving Wiles's masterful portrait of Julia Marlowe (p. 72) is a case in point. If the lady was not born to be an actress, the fact was certainly invented by the painter.

The most obvious theater portraits are those that show the performer in the pursuit of his or her profession. These make up our second category. Here the actor or actress is attired for a favorite role and the dancer dances, while the musician plays, or at least holds, his musical instrument. Peale's portrait of Nancy Hallam shows her in character. She is shown in what we must accept as the actual costume she wore when disguised as the boy Fidele in act 3 of Shakespeare's *Cymbeline*. Peale, however, has placed his painted figure in a very realistic landscape. It is unlike any painted set that would have been seen on the stage in the eighteenth century. In contrast, William Wallace Scott has a century later given us a very faithful rendering of both Edwin Booth's costume for *Hamlet* and the set against which the actor played his part (p. 91). This we know from contemporary photographs of Booth and from detailed watercolor renderings of the *Hamlet* set which now repose in the Harvard Theatre Collection along with Scott's portrait. Frequently, however, the artist has even chosen not to suggest the stage set or any background at all. As in Robert Henri's portrait of Fay Bainter as the Willow Princess (p. 139) and in Guy Pene du Bois's painting of Jeanne Eagels as Sadie Thompson (p. 153), the stance of the actress and the costume evoke the stage.

A third category of theater portraiture is that in which the limits of the stage itself are depicted around the performer. Charles E. Chambers did this deliberately and elaborately in his picture of Josef Hofmann at Carnegie Hall (p. 119). The artist wisely chose to create an interesting picture by depicting the pianist playing an encore. Some of the audience have already moved from their seats in order to rush to their 57th Street buses, and an impatient stage manager or impresario stands in the door leading backstage. In his portrait of the actress Dorothy Stickney (p. 138), John Falter has given us one of the most successful depictions of the two spaces on the stage—the real and the illusionary. With great originality he has shown the actress as Mother Day about to make her entrance in *Life with Father*. She stands in the real space backstage. On her left is the canvas flat which forms the back wall of the set. On her right is the false stairway that rises only so far as to enable it to pass beyond the sight of the theatergoer. At the far right is the illusionary space that the actress is about to enter so that she can play her part. This painting is in every sense a true theater picture.

Dancers pose a much different problem from actors and musicians, and not infrequently the artist has been unsuccessful in suggesting the *magnum mysterium* of their performances. While they have given us images, the lithographers of sheet music covers have seldom evoked for us the capabilities of their subjects (p. 17). The dancers frequently look like awkward marionettes. At best, they look frozen in space and time. The painter Henry Inman solved his problem of painting the dancer Fanny Elssler by depicting her at rest in her dressing room (p. 64). It is also a true theater picture in that it shows a real moment—one that is seldom seen and probably little thought of by the average member of the audience. Toulouse-Lautrec solved the problem of evoking the dance through abstraction. His lithograph of Loïe Fuller (p. 101) abstracts the figure of the dancer into a pattern of curves and plays it off against the dark triangle suggesting the orchestra pit.

The fourth and most unusual category of theater portraiture is the self-portrait. Few indeed are the headliners of the American stage who have practiced it. The earliest we know of are the watercolors by the dancer John Durang (p. 31). These are inserted into the manuscript memoir which he wrote between 1816 and his death in 1822. He shows himself in one double image watercolor as a dwarf turned into a peasant girl. In others, he appears in a sailor suit dancing his famed hornpipe, and in wooden shoes as a Dutch fisherman. He is also seen in kilts dancing a highland fling and in formal dance costume executing a "Pas suel à Vestris."

1, 2. Sheet music covers lithographed by Nathaniel Currier in the 1830s with likenesses of the visiting European dancers Amalia Taglioni and Mlle. Augusta. Both were printed for the firm of Hewitt & Jaques of New York.

The manuscript with its unique watercolors is now in the Historical Society of York County, Pennsylvania.

The singer Enrico Caruso was an accomplished caricaturist, and examples of his work are in many private and public collections. He was fond of drawing his own face (p. 18), but also did innumerable caricatures of fellow musicians in performance and in recording sessions. These drawings are more a collective "portrait" of his own amusement with his profession than anything else. John Barrymore, however, was a much more deliberate caricaturist, and his drawings sometimes served a serious as well as a playful purpose (p. 141). He is said to have frequently drawn himself prior to a new production to see how he might look as a certain character or in a particular makeup. A number of his caricatures are full figure and in color and were presentation items. Playfully, he also often drew his famous profile.

The most recent actor to give serious consideration to self-portraiture was Zero Mostel. One of my more harrowing experiences as a curator was spending two hours with Mostel in his New York studio. I had no choice but to endure his pointed remarks about my typical Anglo-Saxon reserve while I looked at every bit of art he had produced in the year 1970. Not that the art was bad. Most had at least some merit and much was of great interest. The experience was unnerving because of Mostel's manic-comic insistence that I react visibly to each

3. Self-portrait caricature of Enrico Caruso, drawn in New York in 1919.

picture as it was shown. He seemed genuinely proud when I chose the finished oil on canvas of him as John in Eugene Ionesco's *Rhinoceros* (p. 176) for an exhibition at the National Portrait Gallery.

There has never been much of an organized procedure of any kind leading to the execution or production of theater portraiture. From the beginning, it has been a game of "catch as catch can" between artists and actors. Luckily, the performing artist has frequently been greatly admired by painters and sculptors. The most successful portraits have often been those that were created out of the interest of the creative artist in the theater or in a particular production or performer. Charles Willson Peale was quite possibly as enamored of Nancy Hallam as was his neighbor the Rev. Mr. Boucher, who wrote poems to her. Thomas Sully was the son of an actor and actress, and the quality of his few true theater works—gathered together here for the first time (pp. 34, 35, 36, 59)—makes one wish he had painted more of these scene pieces. Aside from the personal interest of the artist, the portrait of a popular performer was thought—often hoped—to be a marketable commodity. It frequently was, and a few sizeable groups of portraits have come into being because of a commercial venture.

The first "collection" of American theater portraits was painted in 1826 for a commercial purpose. In January of that year, the Philadelphia painter John Neagle was hired by Mathias Lopez and Courtney Wemyss to paint a series of small portraits of the leading actors and actresses for twenty-five dollars each. Lopez, who was a prompter in the Philadelphia theater, and his partner Wemyss intended to publish *The Acting American Theatre* as an ongoing series. Each issue would give the text of a popular play, and each was to have an engraved frontispiece of an actor or actress in a role from the play.

According to Wemyss's own memoirs, John Neagle painted a total of twenty-four portraits, of which sixteen were engraved. The first to be issued was that of William Francis as Sir George Thunder, which appeared as the frontispiece to the text of the comedy *Wild Oats* (p. 19). The original portrait of Francis and twelve others from the series are now in the collection of The Players in New York. The group of Neagle portraits is a unique visual document of the nineteenth-century American theater, a painterly performance that features a gala cast: Edmund Keen is seen as Richard III (p. 37), John Duff as Marmion, Mary Duff as Mary (p. 20), Thomas H. Hilson as Tyke (p. 21), Charlotte Barnes as Isabella, John Barnes as Billy Lackaday, Joe Cowell as Crack, James Roberts as Paul Pry, William B. Wood as King

4. William Francis as Sir George Thunder in John O'Keeffe's *Wild Oats*, by John Neagle, 1826. The portrait was engraved by James Barton Longacre and published in *The Acting American Theatre*.

5. Mary Duff as Mary in James Nelson Barker's *Superstition*, by John Neagle, 1826, also engraved by Longacre for *The Acting American Theatre*.

John, John Forrester Foote as Dr. Cantwell, Mrs. William Francis as Miss Harlow, and William Macready as Macbeth.

Not again until the advent of photography were all the headliners of any American theater season so adequately depicted in portraiture, either by painter or printmaker. Among those Neagle portraits missing from the clubhouse of The Players are striking likenesses in costume of two of the brightest stars of the 1826 theater season, Junius Brutus Booth (p. 43) and Edwin Forrest. That of Forrest as Rolla in an English adaptation of Kotzebue's *Pizarro* (p. 21) was the first of many costume pictures of this popular American-born actor to be engraved and circulated among his avid fans.

The miniature sculptures of John Rogers—dubbed "the people's sculptor" by his biographer

David H. Wallace—are also charming visual documents of the American theater, and their creation was prompted both by interest in the drama and by hope of monetary gain. Between 1860 and 1890, Rogers produced about 80,000 small plaster figure groups at an average price of $14.00 each. The groups were a common ornament in many American parlors. Modeled and cast as they were during a heyday of the American theater, it's not surprising that ten of

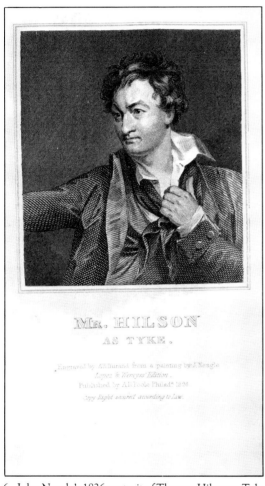

6. John Neagle's 1826 portrait of Thomas Hilson as Tyke in Thomas Morton's *The School of Reform*, as engraved by Asher B. Durand and published in *The Acting American Theatre*.

7. John Neagle's 1826 portrait of Edwin Forrest as Rolla in Kotzebue's *Pizarro*, as engraved by Asher B. Durand and published in *The Acting American Theatre*. The original portrait appears on p. 53.

the groups had themes from the drama (p. 22). Of the ten, eight included portraits of well-known thespians. Three of the eight figures or groups were among the most popular of Rogers's output. Dion Boucicault in the group *Shaughraun and Tatters* (p. 77), and Joseph Jefferson as Bob Acres and as *Rip Van Winkle at Home* (p. 87), seem to have been successful commercially and illustrate the widespread popularity of the two actors with their American audiences.

One of the major monuments of portraiture brought before the public in the twentieth century has also been commercial. In March, 1923, the newsmagazine *Time* began publication. Since that first issue, the magazine has almost always featured on its cover a portrait. In no year has the performing artist been slighted as a newsmaker worthy of attention. The first

8. "Ha! I like not that!" by John Rogers, 1882. This is one of the bronze master models for the group, showing a scene from Shakespeare's *Othello*, act 3, scene 2. Edwin Booth is said to have posed for the figure of Iago, and Tommaso Salvini for the figure of Othello at center.

stage personality to appear on a *Time* cover was Eleanora Duse on July 30, 1923. The second was Ethel Barrymore in November of the following year. The year 1927 saw two performers featured, both singers—Nellie Melba and Geraldine Farrar. In 1929 Walter Hampden, Ina Claire, and Eva Le Gallienne shared the spotlight. The year 1935 was to present five lovely ladies of the stage on *Time* covers. The last two weeks of that year saw two reigning queens of the New York stage back to back. First to appear was Kirsten Flagstad as Isolde, and following her in equally regal splendor was Helen Hayes as Queen Victoria.

From the beginning, *Time* used both photographs and reproductions of drawings, paintings, and other artwork as the source for its cover portraits, so that over the years the magazine amassed a sizeable art collection as well as a photo morgue. Almost a thousand of the original works of art used on *Time* covers have been given to the National Portrait Gallery. Among the more amusing, and a welcome relief from the traditional oil on canvas or watercolor on paper, is a set of large papier-mâché portrait caricatures of the English rock group, The Beatles. Many of the works in the collection are sensitive renderings, both from life and from photos. (See, for example, the portrait of Joan Baez on p. 217.) Whatever one thinks of the overall quality of the portraits, one must admit to it being as valid a compilation of popular portraiture as any archival collection of nineteenth-century sheet music covers with portraits of singers and dancers.

Such commercial ventures into theater portraiture are by and large the exception. More often than not, the creation of a major piece of painting or sculpture with a performer as its subject has been the result of personal contact between artist and actor. Often this contact has been initiated by the artist who greatly admires his sitter-to-be. Sometimes it has been initiated by a third party who wishes to memorialize a favorite star. A personal interest on the part of the creative artist, in addition to talent, of course, is the most important ingredient inherent in the production of a satisfactory portrait.

In our own time there have been several artists who have had a particular interest in the performing arts. Much of their work is represented in this book. The painter Paul Meltsner, for one, has been responsible for a series of paintings of the dancer Martha Graham (p. 174). They seem to have been executed by a combination of personal observation and the use of photographs of the dancer. The painter Edward Biberman (p. 181) and the sculptor Isamu Noguchi (p. 24) also portrayed this famous dancer, and their contact was initially a personal one. The two artists were friends, and Ailes Gilmour, the sister of the sculptor, was in Graham's dance company. Boris Chaliapin, the son of a famous singer father and a ballerina mother, has also taken a particular interest in the theater. His half-size portraits of Alicia Markova (p. 201) and Lucia Chase (p. 193), done with his exacting draftsmanship, are only two of his many portraits of dancers. His notebooks are full of life drawings of his father, Feodor Chaliapin, in most of the roles he sang in the opera house—all drawn from life in the wings or in the dressing room.

Among twentieth-century American sculptors, Richmond Barthé, for one, has modeled a body of theater folk (pp. 183, 189). In early 1947 a group of eighteen of his sculptures were exhibited in New York. The cast of characters included Laurence Olivier as Hotspur, the modern dancer Harald Kreutzberg, and the renowned ecdysiast Gypsy Rose Lee. The small brochure given to visitors to the exhibition at the Grand Central Art Galleries had a one-page essay by the writer-photographer Carl Van Vechten. In it Van Vechten notes that the sculptor preferred to "study his subjects from a chair in the orchestra." While one or two of the sculptures were commissions, most of the sitters seem to have been chosen by Barthé as a result of his attendance at the theater. Herein lies the successful realization inherent in many of his works. He simply loved his subject matter.

9. Martha Graham, bronze head by Isamu Noguchi, 1929.

This volume is intended principally as an entertainment, however feeble a reflection it might be of the pleasures provided audiences by those of the stars that grace its pages. It is obviously neither a scholarly study nor a *catalogue raisonné*. Such a work would have to be in at least several volumes. Some day, perhaps, such a compilation will be undertaken, and rightfully so. The performing artist, as we can see from this brief presentation, has been a subject for painter, sculptor, printmaker, and fabricator of the decorative arts since almost the beginning of stage presentation in the United States, and earlier, of course, elsewhere. As such, the theater portrait is in reality a category of *genre*, and one quite properly suitable for serious study.

This book is based upon an exhibition catalogue which I prepared for the Smithsonian Institution in 1971. The exhibition, *Portraits of the American Stage, 1771-1971*, was shown at the National Portrait Gallery, Smithsonian Institution, as a salute to the inaugural season of The John F. Kennedy Center for the Performing Arts. I am still indebted to all the persons who assisted me in the preparation of the exhibition and to all the individuals and institutions which lent portraits and objects. Many of them have again generously consented to the reproduction of their holdings in this new volume.

Monroe H. Fabian
Washington, D.C.
April, 1980

Charles Willson Peale's portrait of Nancy Hallam is the earliest identifiable portrait of a performer in America that has come down to us. Most of the actors and actresses who came to America before the Revolution exist now only as names in brittle newspapers and playbills and in dry scholarly volumes. Nancy Hallam is one of very few who emerges from these dusty accounts as a real person. Some evidence of her winsome personality and her professional achievements is preserved, but very little is known of her life offstage. There is no record of when and where she was born—presumably in England in the second quarter of the eighteenth century. There is no account of her first appearance in America, but she may have appeared here as early as 1758 playing juvenile roles in the Company of Comedians, managed by David Douglass who was her uncle by marriage.

There is no record of her death, although it may well have occurred in Jamaica where she married the organist of the parish church at Kingston on 15 May 1775. There is ample record, however, to show that she was the first of many players on the American stage to attract a loyal and vociferous following. She can be identified as one of several singers in a concert in St. Philip's Church in Charleston in October of 1765, and there are kind words in that city's press for her performance in *Cinthia* on 4 March 1766. For her benefit performance one month later she acted in the first performance of William Whitehead's *School for Lovers* that was seen in the English colonies. Traveling with Douglass's company, which had been rechristened the American Company of Comedians, she played Annapolis in the autumn of 1770. It was in that city—at the time one of the most genteel centers of life and culture in America—that the most important evidence of her popularity is preserved for us.

Her Imogen in Shakespeare's *Cymbeline* inspired one anonymous correspondent of the *Maryland Gazette* to effusive praise. Printed with his letter were verses extolling the loveliness and talent of the young actress. They proved later to have been written by the Reverend Mr. Jonathan Boucher, rector of St. Ann's parish. Urged on by this extraordinary show of clerical enthusiasm for things secular, Charles Willson Peale painted Nancy Hallam as Imogen in a scene from act 3, scene 6. He chose the moment when Imogen, disguised as the boy Fidele, emerges from a cave where she has been hiding. When Nancy Hallam returned to Annapolis in September and October of 1771, both the real and the counterfeit actresses were available for the admiration of her discriminating public.

Nancy Hallam

10. Nancy Hallam disguised as the boy Fidele in Shakespeare's
Cymbeline, by Charles Willson Peale, 1771. The portrait appears in
color on p. 33.

The most imposing of Thomas Sully's theater portraits is his full-length likeness of George Frederick Cooke in the title role of Shakespeare's *Richard III*. The artist's journal indicates that he began the portrait in April of 1811. It was not listed as finished until 13 June 1812.

George Frederick Cooke had an erratic career of thirty-four years on the English stage before his first appearance in New York on 21 November 1810. His debut role, Richard III, was one of his most successful. His English career had been checkered because of his frequent bouts with the bottle, but when he was sober he was quite frequently a brilliant actor and found a special success in those roles which showed greed and hypocrisy. However these roles may have reflected his own defects of character, he was the first British actor of high professional stature to grace the American stage, and his New York debut was triumphant. Box-office receipts, a major measure of an actor's success, were again very high when he made his first Philadelphia appearances in the following March.

His intemperance caught up with him, however; he died at New York on 26 September 1811 and was buried in the cemetery of St. Paul's Church. In Philadelphia, Thomas Sully's painting of him as Richard III was placed on the shrouded stage of the Chestnut Street Theatre during a special tribute by the company. William B. Wood, manager of the theater, spoke very kindly of Cooke's abilities and personality in his reminiscences published some forty years later. He vouched for the portrait as a true rendering of the actor's costume and facial expression. Edmund Kean, during his visit to America in the second decade of the nineteenth century, had Cooke's body reburied in St. Paul's cemetery beneath a fitting monument. We are told that during the reinterment he took for himself one of George Frederick Cooke's bones which he proudly kept as a relic of a man he considered one of the greatest English actors. He kept it, that is, until Mrs. Kean threw it out.

Shortly after Cooke's death, Sully's great portrait was purchased for $300 by a group of the actor's admirers and presented to the Pennsylvania Academy of the Fine Arts.

George Frederick Cooke, 1756-1811

11. George Frederick Cooke in the title role of Shakespeare's
Richard III, by Thomas Sully, 1811. The portrait appears in color on
p. 34.

John Durang, sometime before his death in 1822, wrote an autobiographical memoir of his life on stage. Added to the volume were six self-portrait watercolors of himself in various roles. He thus became the first of a select handful of performers on the American stage who left first-hand visual as well as written records of themselves.

At various times in his career in the theater John Durang was a dancer, a singer, a mime, a tight-rope walker, a puppeteer, a scene painter, a manager, and an actor. Such theatrical diversity was once commonplace, and he probably had no more varied experience than many other stage-struck young men and women who had been lured by the bright lights of the fledgling American stage. Born in York, Pennsylvania, 6 January 1768, Durang seems to have made his debut in Philadelphia in December of 1784 with Lewis Hallam's company at the Southwark Theatre. The Revolutionary War was still an unpleasant memory that reflected against the largely English company, and so John Durang, the only native-born member of the group, was singled out for applause. His favorite contribution to an evening's entertainment seems to have been dancing the hornpipe.

In August of 1785 the Hallam company opened in New York where Durang was billed as Scaramouche in a harlequinade, *The Touchstone, or Harlequin Traveler*. His famous hornpipe remained, however, both his and his audiences' favorite. After a season in New York, Durang was back in Philadelphia giving puppet plays in his family's house. In 1778 Durang joined Hallam's Old American Company again for seven years of touring. Early in the 1790s he was overshadowed by the talents of European-trained dancers who began to appear on American stages. In 1794 Durang performed an Indian dance in the premiere of *Tammany*, one of the first American operas with a native subject. The critics are silent as to the merits of our hero's contribution. At his benefit performance on 11 June 1794, Durang performed for the first time on the slack wire and may also have been the choreographer of the pantomime *The Huntress, or Tammany's Frolics*, which enshrined this astounding performance. He was all the while still dancing the hornpipe at the slightest provocation. In 1796 he was a secondary dancer with the ballet company of Jean-Baptiste Francisque which attached itself to the Old American Company. From October 1796 until December of 1799 Durang performed with John B. Rickett's Circus in Philadelphia and New York. The following summer he became co-impresario with John B. Rowson at the Southwark Theatre.

From that time on until his retirement from the stage in 1819, he was a member of the stock company of Philadelphia's Chestnut Street Theatre during the winter seasons. In the summers between 1808 and 1816 he formed his own company and toured the rural areas of Pennsylvania and Maryland. He was the star of his Pennsylvania-German dialect productions of Shakespeare's *Taming of the Shrew* and *Richard III*. He retired from the stage in 1819 and settled permanently in Philadelphia, where he died on 29 March 1822.

John Durang, 1768-1822

12, 13. Two of the self-portrait watercolors from John Durang's autograph memoirs. The first shows him dancing the hornpipe. The artist-actor carefully indicated the scenery on the narrow stage. The second watercolor shows him in a quick-change act of a dwarf who turns into a maiden.

Abandoned by his mother shortly after his birth out of wedlock on 4 November 1787, Edmund Kean rose literally from the gutters of London to one of the most prominent positions in the history of his profession. He is said to have begun his stage career at age three impersonating Cupid, and, whatever the facts of his early career on the stage might be, we do know that his first appearance as Shylock in *The Merchant of Venice* at Drury Lane on 26 January 1814 is an event of exceptional importance in the annals of the drama in England. So powerful were his characterizations of this and other roles he essayed that season that the management cleared an unprecedented £20,000 in four months. Benjamin West, this country's first expatriate painter, is said to have avowed that Kean's facial expression in *Richard III* kept him awake all night. We take that comment to be one great artist's praise for another. The theatergoing public was as fickle then as it is now, however, and waning interest in England was no doubt part of the reason Kean elected to undertake a tour of the United States in 1820.

His first American appearance was as *Richard III* with the Park Theatre Company at New York's Anthony Street Theatre on 29 November. He was, of course, a success, even though the newspapers took prejudiced stands for and against him. He appeared to great applause in Philadelphia, and William B. Wood in his *Recollections* credits Kean with instituting the theater custom we now accept as the prerogative of all dramatic artists, worthy or unworthy both—the final bow at the end of the play. With little sympathy for the ceremony, Wood wrote, "The absurdity of dragging out before the curtain a deceased Hamlet, Macbeth, or Richard in an exhausted state, merely to take a bow . . . is one which we date from this time."

Shortly after beginning a second engagement in Boston on 23 May 1821, Kean refused to play before a light audience. The local newspapers were indignant and the attitude echoed in New York and Philadelphia. Kean canceled the remainder of his scheduled tour and returned to England, justified, however, in considering his American tour an unqualified dramatic success. Back home he became the object of public scorn when named a co-defendant in a notorious divorce case, and he left again for a tour of the United States.

News of his English nocturnal adventures preceded him, and he was treated as a villain by the American press. His second New York debut on 14 November 1825, again as Richard III, was greeted with both hisses and cheers, and the remainder of his thirteen-month tour was to be punctuated with the same declamations. He considered his election as a chief of the Huron tribe in Quebec the highlight of his American career. He had visiting cards printed with "Edmund Kean" on one side and his Indian name, "Alanienouidet," on the other. His last American appearance was in New York on 5 December 1826. Upon his return to England, his career and his health declined steadily. On 12 March 1833 he collapsed on the stage at Drury Lane and died on 15 May.

John Neagle's portrait of Edmund Kean appears on p. 37.

Edmund Kean, 1787-1833

I. Nancy Hallam as Imogen in William Shakespeare's *Cymbeline* by Charles Willson Peale, 1771. The actress is shown in a moment from act 3, scene 6, when Imogen, disguised as a boy, emerges from the cave where she has been hiding.

II. George Frederick Cooke in the title role of William Shakespeare's *Richard III* by Thomas Sully, 1811. Sully's second and greatest theater portrait was begun in April, 1811, and was not finished until June of the next year. After the actor's death, it was bought by admirers and presented to the Pennsylvania Academy of the Fine Arts.

III. Edwin Forrest in the title role of John Augustus Stone's *Metamora* by Frederick Styles Agate, probably 1830. The play, first performed in December of 1829, won a prize offered by the actor for an American play.

IV. William Burke Wood as Charles de Moor in Joseph Holman's adaptation of Friedrich Schiller's *The Robbers* by Thomas Sully, 1811. The painting is the artist's first major work on a theatrical subject.

V. Mary Ann Wood as Amina in Sir Henry Bishop's English adaptation of Vincenzo Bellini's *La Sonnambula*, by Thomas Sully, 1836. Shown is a moment in the second sleepwalking scene near the end of the opera. In the background is the bass William Francis Brough as Count Rodolfo. The painting has been cut down, and the tenor Joseph Wood is now missing from the background.

14. Edmund Kean in the title role of Shakespeare's *Richard III*, by
John Neagle, 1826.

Thomas Sully painted three of the finest early nineteenth-century portraits of performing artists. The first of these was his painting of William Burke Wood. Wood is shown as Charles de Moor in Joseph Holman's adaptation of Friedrich Schiller's *Die Räauber*, or *The Robbers*. The character of de Moor is shown in the camp of the brigands at sunrise. The portrait was begun in Philadelphia on 10 August 1810 and not finished until June of the following year.

The stage debut of Montreal-born William Burke Wood took place in Annapolis in 1798. It occurred with a touring company managed by Thomas Wignell, and in December of that year Wood appeared for the first time with them on their home stage in Philadelphia. His career in the City of Brotherly Love was to last forty-eight years and thus encompass the most important formative period of the infant American theater.

In 1810 he became co-manager of the Chestnut Street Theatre with his fellow actor, William Warren, and this association was to continue until 1826 when for a brief while he served as manager of the rival Arch Street Theatre. Leaving managership behind, he continued to act with various companies until his farewell on the stage of Philadelphia's Walnut Street Theatre on 18 November 1846. Wood published in 1855 his *Personal Recollections of the Stage*, a treasury of information concerning dramatic history and practice in America in the first half of the last century. He quotes no glowing reviews of his own performances, except for a justifiably detailed description of the farewell tendered to him in 1846. As an afterthought he cites his prodigious record of characterizations— 342 roles in 199 plays—each born, no doubt, more of the ever-present necessity which lightly cloaked the actors on the adolescent American stage, than any manifestation of dramatic genius.

William Dunlap, the most proficient chronicler of the early nineteenth-century stage in the United States, found Wood's greatest ability in what we today would call drawing-room comedy, and then added, "he succeeds admirably well in tragedy, too." William Burke Wood died in Philadelphia on 23 September 1861.

William Burke Wood, 1779-1861

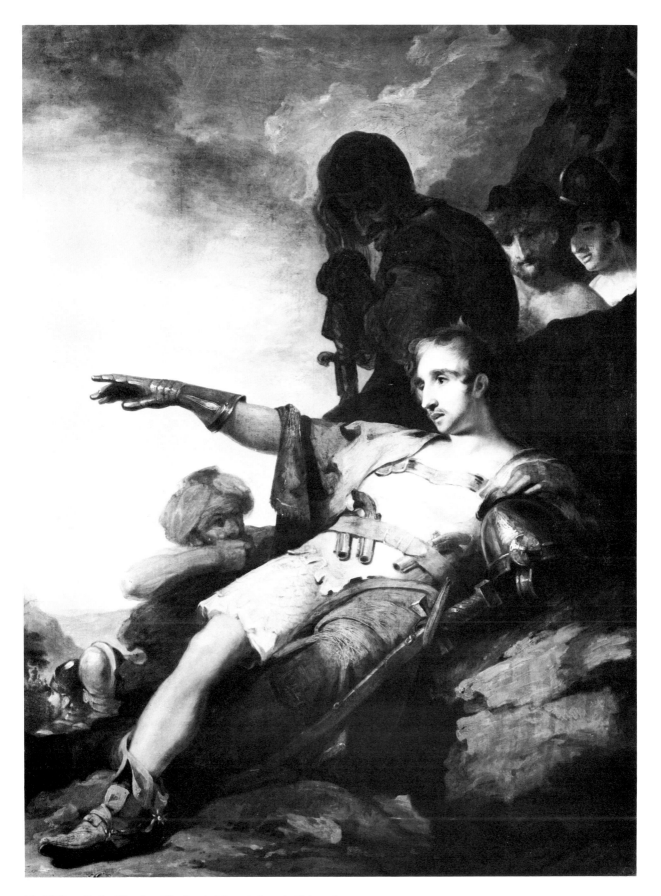

15. William Burke Wood as Charles de Moor in Joseph Holman's
The Robbers, by Thomas Sully, 1811. This portrait appears in color
on p. 34.

During the sixteen years he had appeared on English stages prior to his first appearance in New York's Park Theatre on 2 October 1826, William Charles Macready had risen slowly and steadily to the highest rank of his profession. Playbills announced him as "That Eminent Tragedian," and, despite a reputation among his colleagues for unpleasantness and egotism, he was a favorite with critics and public alike. The completeness of his characterizations and the evenness of his performance from first curtain to last came as a welcome relief from the usual bombastic declamation of his time. During his first American tour he was being paid twice what his presence commanded at London's Drury Lane, and by the time he acted his last performance of *Macbeth* at the Park on 4 June 1827, he had amassed both considerable reputation and profit from his new audiences. He returned to England, and considered eventual retirement in the promising New World. He returned again in September of 1843 for a lengthy second American tour.

This time around his success was dampened by the growing hostility of Edwin Forrest, who initiated a lengthy feud based upon merest suspicion. (See page 52.) His audiences still appreciated his efforts, however, and he went home thirteen months later £5,500 richer than when he had come. On 4 October 1848, he began a farewell tour of the United States with a performance of *Macbeth* at Niblo's Astor Place Opera House in New York. One of the Boston newspapers had greeted him viciously upon his arrival for this tour, and he unwisely made a curtain speech in reply to the attack. It was taken as a challenge by the overly chauvinistic members of the Native American political party and by Edwin Forrest's staunchest fans who included among their number many disreputable Bowery types. Toward the end of his farewell tour, Macready appeared again at the Astor Place on 7 May 1849. Abuse and chairs from the gallery rained down on him and the actor was forced to terminate the performance.

Placated by a visiting committee of New York supporters, he attempted to act again three days later. An unruly mob of ten to fifteen thousand assembled outside the theater along with sizeable detachments from the New York police and militia. In the inevitable riot which ensued about thirty people were killed. Macready was forced to flee the city in disguise, although his role in the disgraceful affair had merely been that of innocent catalyst. He returned to England having discarded any idea of retiring in the United States and was convinced, as were many others, of Edwin Forrest's disgraceful importance as an instigator, if not the mastermind, of the disastrous Astor Place riot.

William Charles Macready, 1793-1873

16. William Charles Macready in the title role of James Sheridan Knowles's *William Tell*, by Henry Inman, about 1827.

Junius Brutus Booth made his stage debut at an amateur theater in London in 1813. Within two years he was engaged for a season at Covent Garden. On 12 February 1817 he appeared again at Covent Garden, and after two performances of *Richard III* found himself unjustly accused as an imitator of Edmund Kean. At age twenty-one he was suddenly the center of theatrical gossip and the cause of at least two theater riots because of his alleged Kean impersonations. Personally, he seems to have been on good terms with his eminent rival, however, for twice, in February of 1817 and on 7 August 1820, he played Iago to Kean's *Othello*.

In January of 1821 Booth married, and traveling by way of France and Madeira, sailed to America with his new bride. On 6 July he made his American debut at Richmond, Virginia, and on 5 October 1821 he appeared at the Park Theatre in New York for the first time. Obviously intending to stay in the New World, he acquired a tract of land near Bel Air, Maryland, where he built a small house and began to raise his family, three of whom, Junius Brutus, Jr., Edwin, and John Wilkes, were to make their mark on American history. Aside from short visits to England in 1825 and 1836, his career from 1821 on was an American career. He attained popularity swiftly. Walt Whitman, looking back at the first decade of the Bowery Theatre, which had opened in October of 1826, saw it as existing strictly as a showcase for the performances of two actors, Edwin Forrest and Junius Brutus Booth. Being a capable linguist—Booth spoke German, Dutch, and French and had once played Shylock with a Yiddish accent—he may well have been the first American actor to perform in any other than his native language. In 1828 while in New Orleans as the stage manager of Camp Street Theatre, he acted Oreste in Racine's *Andromaque* in French at the neighboring Theatre d'Orleans.

In 1831 he assumed for a while the management of the Adelphi Theatre in Baltimore. He began about this time, unfortunately, to exhibit the symptoms of a deranged mind, but he remained a favorite with audiences as far afield as Boston and New Orleans. In Mobile he acted with young Joseph Jefferson III. In his autobiography, Jefferson tells of Booth's ability to assume and drop his character at will and of performances so intense that the audience was stunned into silence and could not applaud. In 1852 he joined his sons Edwin and Junius Brutus, Jr., in a tour of California. Leaving them, he traveled eastward and played at the Charles Street Theatre in New Orleans what was to be his final engagement. His last appearance on any stage was on 19 November 1852. He died eleven days later on board a steamboat bound for Cincinnati.

John Neagle's portrait of Booth in the title role of John Howard Payne's *Brutus* was painted in 1827, shortly after the opening of the Bowery Theatre.

Junius Brutus Booth, 1796-1852

17. Junius Brutus Booth in the title role of John Howard Payne's
Brutus, by John Neagle, 1827.

In 1823 Henry Inman exhibited the earliest known painting of any scene from Washington Irving's "Rip Van Winkle." It's not surprising, then, that he would eventually paint the actor James Henry Hackett as Rip Van Winkle in Hackett's adaptation of the Irving story. First performed in New York in 1830, *Rip Van Winkle* was the most successful adaptation of the story for the stage prior to that of Joseph Jefferson in 1865. Jefferson, it is said, thought of Hackett as always being an amateur at theatricals, but some of his countemporaries were kinder.

The author of Hackett's obituary which appeared in the *New York Tribune* on the day after his death in 1871 said of his Rip Van Winkle that it was a "marvelously strong representation of the commonplace, good-natured, vagabound." He added, however, that he felt Jefferson had wafted the character into the "higher realm of the ideal." Inman, the artist, seems also to have appreciated the actor, for his portrait is one of the most vigorous he did of theatrical folk. It shows Rip, upon awakening, discovering his old flintlock lifted up high by a tree not there when he fell asleep.

It was pointed out in the obituary that Hackett also had the dubious honor of having been the manager of the Astor Place Theatre during the Forrest-Macready riot of 1849. The writer also correctly recognized Hackett's importance in the development of the comedy character based upon American types. There were those who thought that Hackett's Falstaff, which he acted for three decades in both Shakespearean plays in which the comic character appears, was his finest characterization. Many in his audiences, however, almost certainly enjoyed even more the antics of such native star-spangled characters as Uncle Ben, Melodious Migrate, and the unpolished freshman congressman, Colonel Nimrod Wildfire.

18. *Opposite page:* James Henry Hackett in the awakening scene from *Rip Van Winkle,* by Henry Inman, 1830.

James Henry Hackett, 1800-1871

The ballet *La Sylphide*, with choreography by Filippo Taglioni and music by Jean Schneitzhoeffer, was first performed in Paris in 1832 and marked the beginning of the romantic age of the dance. Fragments of the ballet had been performed in the United States from 1835 on, and its first complete performance was given in New York's Park Theatre on 22 May 1839. The occasion was the American debut of Paul Taglioni, son of the choreographer, and his wife, Amalia Galster Taglioni. Paul Taglioni had acquired a notable reputation as a dancer and ballet master, and, since he and his wife were among the first European dancers of note to come to the United States, it is understandable that they were well received.

Three days after their debut, the *New York Literary Gazette* reported that "Madame Taglioni is remarkable for the peculiar ease, as well as the grace and elegance of her movements; many of her figures and steps are entirely new to a New York audience. Nor is Mons. Taglioni less excellent in his art—perhaps of the two, he is the best dancer; a symmetrical figure adds greatly to the pleasure which his performance gives; he is entirely free from the buffoonery which generally distinguishes male dancers of the French ballet . . . ."

The Taglionis were in this country for only five months. After their May performances in New York they appeared in Philadelphia, took a July vacation to Niagara Falls, and closed their American engagement by appearing again at the Park in August and September. On 2 October 1839 they took ship for London. During their relatively short stay they had firmly planted one of the most important and durable ballet classics in American taste and had sowed the seeds of enthusiasm for the dance which were to blossom less than a year later with the arrival of Fanny Elssler.

Paul Taglioni, 1808-1884
Amalia Taglioni, 1801-1881

19. A rare New York lithograph of the early days of ballet in that city, featuring Paul Taglioni as James and Amalia Taglioni in the title role of *La Sylphide*. It was published by H. R. Robinson in 1839.

When Mary Ann Wood made her American debut at the Park Theatre in New York as Cinderella on 19 September 1833, she had already held title for some years to the claim of being one of England's finest singers. In 1822, at age nineteen, she was fully established professionally when she appeared at London's Covent Garden as Mandane in Arne's opera *Artaxerxes*.

In the United States she will always be associated with the role of Amina in Vincenzo Bellini's opera *La Sonnambula*. She and her tenor husband, Joseph Wood, first introduced the opera to the American public in New York, in English during the early part of the season of 1835-1836. They repeated the opera eleven times with great success in Boston—where Mrs. Wood also found time to encourage a young singer named Charlotte Cushman—and then brought it to Philadelphia. Here the *United States Gazette* ran a laudatory column on 11 February 1836, the day scheduled for the first performance. We do not know who the author of the column may have been, but if he was not a public relations man in the pay of the Woods, he certainly should have been. A short excerpt will suffice to show off his talent:

> An Italian, who was the personal friend of Bellini, thus writes from Boston:—'Last night I went to hear La Sonnambula by Bellini!—which I heard at home, two days before I went away. Mrs. Wood sings it like an angel (come un'angelo!) she sings and acts it *with her soul*. She would astonish, delight, and make crazy, an Italian audience. Per Dio! che musica! and what singing!' . . . If, then, gentle reader, thou wouldst enjoy an elevating pastime, and refresh thyself with a refining pleasure, go and hear La Sonnambula. If thou art old, the dreams of youth will again come o'er thee—if thou are young, the depth and sanctity of thy feelings will be revealed to thee,—if thou are care-worn, tranquility will visit thy weary breast; if thou art immersed in the world's business, better moments will cheer thee;—if thou hast a human heart, and would have its foun-tains stirred, and thy spirit soothed, agitated and renewed—go—go—gentle reader—go and hear La Sonnambula.

So great was the response of the Philadelphia music-loving public that the opera was performed every night but Sunday from the eleventh until the twenty-sixth of February. The future of roman-tic opera in America was assured by this remarkable marathon of bel canto singing. It should be noted, however, that to make certain the audience went away satisfied, each night's performance of the opera was capped with lighter entertainment. Let us hope that those who did not succumb to the pathos of *La Sonnambula* did at least enjoy the performances of those timeless favorites *Freaks and Follies*, *Forty Winks*, and *The Twa Ghaists*. Mary Ann Wood appeared intermittently in the United States until 1841, quite frequently to the tune of her husband's business disagreements with various theater managers.

The Woods' last appearance in America was in a production of Bellini's *Norma* in an English translation by Joseph R. Fry. It opened at Philadelphia's Chestnut Street Theatre on 11 January 1841 and was sung for the last time on 4 February. Four days later the Woods sailed for England vowing in a press announcement never to return.

With them they took both Thomas Sully's study for Mary Ann in the role of Amina in *La Son-nambula* and the large finished painting of a scene from the finale of the opera. The large painting had been commissioned by the manager of the Chestnut Street Theatre in Philadelphia and was given to the Woods as part settlement for fees owed them.

Mary Ann Wood, 1802-1864

20. Thomas Sully's study for his large portrait of Mary Ann Wood
as Amina in Bellini's *La Sonnambula*, 1836. The portrait itself appears
in color on p. 36.

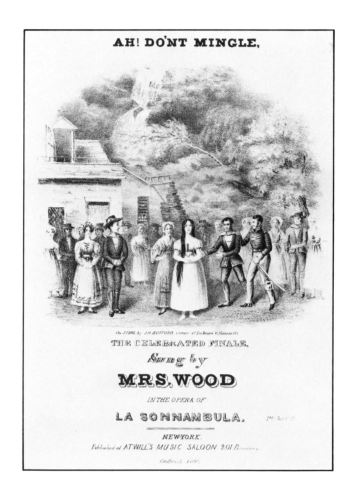

21, 22. Illustrated covers for sheet music published in New York as the result of Mary Ann Wood's successes in Italian opera, about 1836.

ON YONDER ROCK RECLINING,

from Auber's Grand Opera

OF

FRADIAVOLO

As Sung by

MR. & MRS. WOOD.

Edwin Forrest's first attempts at theatricals were made on the stage of the South Street Theatre in his native Philadelphia when he was eleven years old. His professional debut was made only three years later, on 27 November 1820, in the same city's Walnut Street Theatre; he then served an apprenticeship in small theaters on the frontier, playing in towns along the Ohio and Mississippi rivers as far south as New Orleans. In 1825 he was acting in Albany where he played Iago to Edmund Kean's Othello. On 23 June 1826, with an audacity that was very much part of his nature, he made his New York debut in the Park Theatre playing the role that had been Kean's the season before. He was a great success and was hired by the Bowery Theatre where his characterizations and his vigorous manner of declamation endeared him to the downtown audiences. After five seasons at the Bowery, Forrest was engaged by the Park Theatre.

While there, he encouraged the writing of plays with American subjects, offering prizes to their authors. Both John A. Stone's *Metamora*, first produced on 15 December 1829, and Robert M. Bird's *The Gladiator*, premiered on 15 September 1831, were to remain among the most popular of Forrest's stage creations throughout his career. In 1834 he retired temporarily from the stage in his native land to travel in Europe and to make his London debut. His strong personality and the passion of his acting won enthusiastic audiences for him there, too, and he became the first American to achieve success both in his native country and abroad. He also took time out from the rigors of recreation and of profession to fall in love and to marry Catharine Norton Sinclair in the English capital on 23 June 1837. Fittingly, the clergyman presiding at the marriage was Henry Hart Milman, author of the melodrama *Fazio*, a play beloved on both sides of the Atlantic.

In 1845 Forrest visited England for the second time. Ill received by hissing claques during a London appearance as Macbeth, he comprehended the incident as the work of his English rival William Charles Macready and returned the favor by hissing the British actor at a performance of *Hamlet* in Edinburgh on 2 March 1846. Forrest then arrogantly admitted the action in a letter submitted to the London *Times* and began a controversy which was to culminate in New York in the Astor Place riot of 10 May 1849. Forrest's reputation was sullied by the affair, but he remained in favor with those audiences which saw him as a champion of native Americanism. Two years later his name was again paraded by the press for off-stage performances when he and his wife sued each other for divorce.

From 1852 on he frequently went into self-imposed retirement. In 1860 he reappeared with great success in New York and Boston as Hamlet, and in 1866, although laboring with partial paralysis, he played to record audiences in Chicago and San Francisco. His last appearance was in Boston on 7 December 1872. Upon his death in Philadelphia five days later, it ws discovered that he had left his entire estate for the founding of a home for retired actors.

23. *Opposite page:* Edwin Forrest as Rolla in Richard Brinsley Sheridan's adaptation of A. F. F. von Kotzebue's *Pizarro*, by John Neagle, 1826.

Edwin Forrest, 1806-1872

24. Sheet music for a march composed in Edwin Forrest's honor, 1851.

Ira Aldridge was the first native-born American actor to win international recognition. Born in New York on 27 July 1807, he probably acted for the first time in the African Theatre on Mercer Street.

In 1824 or 1825 he went to England, and, billed as "Mr. Keene," his earliest documented appearance on stage occurred as Oroonoko in *The Revolt of Surinam* at London's Royal Coburg Theatre on 10 October 1825. The critics' reviews ran the gamut from praise to ridicule. The writer for the *Times* allowed that "It is very difficult to criticize a black actor, on account of the novelty of the spectacle . . . ," and then went on to describe a performance that he said was characterized by "rant and affectation." *The Morning Adviser*, however, found the eighteen-year-old actor's performance "a very excellent conception of the character." On 17 December 1825 Ira Aldridge played Othello for the first time at the Theatre Royal in Brighton, and exactly two years later he had gained sufficient reputation to win his first official international recognition in the form of an honorary commission in the Grenadier Guards of the President of Haiti. The West Indian nation honored him for his London performance in *The Death of Christophe*, a play about the Haitian struggle for independence.

In December of 1831 he reached one of the high points of his early career when he was seen in Dublin by Edmund Kean and recommended by him to the manager of the Theatre Royal in Bath. By the spring of 1833, when he played Othello for the first time at London's Covent Garden on 10 April, he had shed his false name and was now appearing as "Mr. Aldridge" and as "The African Roscius," Roscius, of course, having been one of the greatest actors in classical Rome. He had also acquired the animosity of the proslavery group which controlled the managements of the fashionable London West End theaters and was in effect banned from them after his second performance at Covent Garden. For the next nineteen years he stayed primarily in the provinces. Notable successes during these years were his appearances in the title role of *Fabian the Mulatto*, and his own adaptation of Shakespeare's *Titus Andronicus*, purged of all its gore and unpleasantness. It was the first production of the play in 128 years, and Aldridge took the opportunity also to rework the character of Aaron, who he played, from a black villain to a black hero. On 28 April 1851 he played a performance of *Othello* in the Shakespeare Theatre at Stratford-upon-Avon. By April of 1852 some of the less prejudiced critics of the London press were calling him "a star of the first magnitude."

In July of 1852 he left for his first tour of the Continent. Except for a short engagement at the Haymarket Theatre in London in the summer of 1865, he was never again to act in England. From his first appearance in Europe until his last he was passionately received by all who saw him. After seeing his Othello, the *Preussische Zeitung* called him "the most beautiful male artist that one can imagine." The famous French critic Theophile Gautier, having seen him in St. Petersburg, described Aldridge's acting as "a majestically classical style much resembling that of Macready" and considered his King Lear, one of the roles he played in "white-face," an even better performance than his famed Othello. Frederick William IV presented him with the gold medal of the Prussian Academy of Arts and Sciences, an award made previously only to Baron von Humboldt, Franz Liszt, and the composer Gasparo Spontini. He was knighted by Duke Bernhard of Saxe-Meiningen; given the White Cross of Switzerland by the City of Berne; and, among other honors, was granted an honorary membership in the Imperial Academy of Beaux Arts of Russia, where he was a special favorite of audiences and fellow actors from 1858 on. In March of 1866 he became the first actor to perform Shakespeare in English in Constantinople.

Ira Aldridge, 1807-1867

He was planning a tour of America when he died at Lodz, Poland, on 7 August 1867. He was buried there with full civil and military honors, and his grave is now cared for by the Society of Polish Artists of Film and Theatre.

25. *Above:* Ira Aldridge as Mungo in *The Padlock*, an engraving published by John Tallis in London, 1850 or 1851.

26. *Opposite page:* Ira Aldridge as Othello, by Henry Perronet Briggs, about 1830. This portrait appears in color on p. 70.

As the heiress to the talent of one of England's leading theatrical families—she was the niece of John Philip Kemble and Sarah Siddons and the daughter of Charles Kemble—Fanny Kemble made her debut onstage when her family needed her. On 5 October 1829 she made her first appearance as Juliet at Covent Garden in a successful effort to save her father from financial ruin. She never liked acting, and she was rather condescending in her attitude toward most in her profession.

On 18 September 1832 she appeared for the first time in the United States when she acted Bianca in Henry Hart Milman's *Fazio* at the Park Theatre in New York. Her manner offstage was quite often haughty and her performances onstage were uneven, but she charmed her American audiences sufficiently to be an immediate and grand success. Although the *United States Gazette* gave much more coverage to the Italian opera, then popular in the City of Brotherly Love, and to Edwin Forrest's exploits at the Arch Street Theatre, the newspaper prepared Philadelphia for her debut in that city by quoting reviews as early as two days after her first performance in New York: "The New York Enquirer of yesterday says—Miss Fanny Kemble made her first appearance last evening . . . . As an actress she stands unrivalled before the American public; and never have we seen one who can compare with her."

By the time she finally appeared in Philadelphia, the theatergoing public was well disposed to receive her with open arms. After her performance as Belvedera in *Venice Preserved* the correspondent of the *Gazette* wrote on 24 October 1832, "It was the first opportunity we have had to view the latter [Fanny] in Tragedy, and, to us, her offerings at the shrine of Melpomene, were more acceptable than those presented to her gay laughter-loving sister." Her Bianca was again admired as was her Julia in *The Hunchback*. Of the dozen or so portraits of her painted by Philadelphia's premier artist Thomas Sully, eight were painted between 1832 and 1834. One shows her as Juliet, one as Bianca, and one as Beatrice. In 1833 Sully noted that he rubbed out one he had started of her as Lady Macbeth. The Sully portraits alone would be a stunning record of Fanny's popularity with her American public.

Her Washington debut was attended by Dolley Madison and John Quincy Adams. John Marshall and Joseph Story came often to see her while she was in the capital, and she was even presented to President Jackson at the White House. In Philadelphia she had met an eligible young—and rich—bachelor named Pierce Butler. He persistently followed her on her tours, sometimes playing the flute in theater orchestras to be near her. She eventually succumbed to his wooing, and on 7 June 1834 they were married in Philadelphia's Christ Church. It was the end of her short career in America, for two weeks later she acted her farewell performance in the aptly chosen *The Wedding Day* at the Chestnut Street Theatre. Her married life, however, was not happy, and she left her husband and returned to England.

In February of 1847 she went back again to the stage, but as before, she found it distasteful. The following spring she held her first readings of Shakespeare from a lecture platform. Finding this method of reaching her audiences less objectionable than assuming a character in costume, it was how she chose to appear in public until her last public reading in 1869. Her husband having died in 1867, Fanny spent the remainder of her life visiting with daughters in England and in Germantown, Pennsylvania. She died in London on 15 January 1893.

Fanny Kemble, 1809-1893

27. Fanny Kemble as Bianca in Henry Hart Milman's *Fazio*, by Thomas Sully, 1833.

Clara Fisher began her professional career at age six on the stage of London's Drury Lane Theatre, appearing in both the play *Lilliput* and part of the fifth act of *Richard III*. She toured throughout England as a child actress and spent three years as a member of the professional company at the Drury Lane just prior to her coming to America.

Her debut at New York's Park Theatre in 1827 was as Albina Mandeville in a play called *The Will*. The ballad "Hurrah for the Bonnets of Blue," which she introduced into the play to enliven her part, had an electrifying effect upon her audience and was forever associated with her. As a young and pretty actress she was well received, and women young and old who thought themselves fashionable imitated her hair style and her lisp. She was painted by both Chester Harding and Henry Inman; the latter portrayed her wearing her armlet mounted with a miniature of George Frederick Cooke.

Although she seems to have had a rather limited vocal range, she ventured into opera with pleasing results. Her singing of John Howard Payne's "Home, Sweet Home" in Sir Henry Bishop's musical setting from his opera *Clari; or the Maid of Milan* was one of those magical moments in the history of the theater that always moved audiences to tears. In 1834 she married James Gaspard Maeder, vocal coach of the visiting English singers Mary Ann and Joseph Wood. As "Mrs. Maeder" she appeared on opera bills throughout the country. At one significant performance in Boston on 8 April 1835, she sang Susanna in a production of Mozart's *The Marriage of Figaro* that marked the stage debut of a young local singer named Charlotte Cushman. In a manner of gilding the lily typical of the times, the Mozart was topped off with a performance of a comic opera called *Pet of the Petticoats* with Mrs. Maeder in the role of Poll the Pet.

Mrs. Maeder's popularity waned with her youth, but she remained on the American stage for sixty years, playing roles ranging from light comedy to Shakespearean tragedy. In 1843, with the cooperation of John Sefton, she introduced musical theatricals in the Boston Museum, and in the fall of 1845 she was one of the first members of the stock company of Boston's Howard Athenaeum. She also continued to appear on the New York stage, one notable occasion being the 1865 performance of *School for Scandal* which opened Lucy Rushton's Theatre. Clara Fisher Maeder's last appearance on stage was in Baltimore in 1889 as Mrs. Jeremiah Joblots in Augustin Daly's *Lottery of Love*. She died in Metuchen, New Jersey, at the home of her daughter-in-law on 12 November 1898.

Clara Fisher, 1811-1898

28. Clara Fisher, by Henry Inman, 1828.

62

29. Candelabra with a figure of
Fanny Elssler dancing the
Cachucha.

Fanny Elssler was twenty-nine years old and near the peak of her career when Stephan Price, co-manager of the Park Theatre, met her in Paris in the autumn of 1839 and persuaded her to contract for her first American appearances. Left the sole proprietor of the Park by Price's death some months later, Edmund Simpson almost canceled the contract for fear that she would be received with little enthusiasm and with loss rather than profit. He could not have been more wrong. Being the first European ballerina to contemplate a tour of America, Fanny Elssler was eagerly awaited. The New York press, notably the *New York Morning Herald*, paved the way to her New World success with glittering reviews of her personal accomplishments and her professional triumphs. The first issue of the *Spirit of the Times*, published after her Park Theatre debut on 14 May 1840, described in the florid prose of the period the scene when she appeared onstage: "The celebrated dance of *La Cracovienne* followed, and brought the fair debutante before the public at a bound! The time-honored walls of Old Drury never echoed with more tumultuous, deafening plaudits. The pit rose *en masse*—hats and handkerchiefs waved in every direction." And after she had danced her second number of the evening, the ballet *La Tarentule*, "she was called for with a degree of enthusiasm unprecedented in the theatrical annals of this country."

The mass hysteria that began that night in New York was to follow her through most of her appearances during her twenty-six month tour of the United States and Cuba. Philadelphia saw her for the first time a month later and, among other honors paid her, produced a cast-metal candelabra base depicting her in the costume of her famed Spanish dance, *La Cachucha*. She was also to be immortalized in the swiftly produced covers of lithographed sheet music and in a lovely portrait by Henry Inman. The New York artist wisely chose to represent her at rest in her dressing room at the Park rather than as dancing.

On 11 July 1840 she appeared for the first time in Washington, and Congress adjourned early so that its members could be in attendance. Having attended her third performance in the capital city

Fanny Elssler, 1810-1884

LA CRACOVIENNE,

AS DANCED BY

FANNY ELSSLER.

N.YORK. Published by FIRTH & HALL, N°1, Franklin Square
239 Broadway

30. Fanny Elssler on the cover of the sheet music for her dance *La Cracovienne*, published in New York in 1841 or 1842.

in the company of his entire Cabinet, President Martin Van Buren invited her to the White House the following morning. Tongues wagged at the disgrace of a dancer being received at the White House. In Baltimore she was at first coolly received, but, after her second performance, the horses were unharnessed from her carriage and jubilant male fans drew the carriage and their new idol to her hotel. Boston was determined not to follow the example of the other cities, but soon capitulated to her talent and her personality. Emerson and Longfellow were charmed by her. Half the city found her benefit for the Bunker Hill Monument Fund a gracious response to their hospitality, while the other half expressed indignation that the earnings of a foreign ballet dancer should be so used. Richmond was more appreciative when she agreed to dance an unscheduled performance there. The Governor of Virginia escorted her on a visit to the state capitol, and she was borne there from her hotel on a litter carried on the shoulders of six state senators.

When she first appeared in Havana in January of 1841, she was paid the unprecedented sum of $1,000 a night. In April she appeared in New Orleans, where wreaths of strawberries joined the usual wreaths of flowers flung onstage at the end of a performance. The second year of her tour was spoiled slightly by malicious stories about her in the press, but she went on her triumphant peregrination of American theaters as the queen she was. By the end of her tour she had danced 208 performances and had supposedly earned nearly $140,000. Much of this was given to charity. Her last performance in America, a benefit for the Theatrical Fund, was danced at the Park Theatre on 1 July 1842.

She sailed for Europe from New York on 16 July, on board the *Caledonia*. As the steamer left the harbor, the band in the ship-of-the-line *Ohio* played "America" and "La Cracovienne" in farewell. Fanny Elssler danced for the last time in Vienna on 21 June 1851 and died there on 27 November 1884.

31. Fanny Elssler in her dressing room at the Park Theatre, by
Henry Inman, 1841.

Charlotte Cushman was an eighteen-year-old contralto in the choir of Ralph Waldo Emerson's Boston church when the visiting English prima donna Mary Ann Wood encouraged her to pursue a career in grand opera. Consequently, Charlotte made her debut on 8 April 1835 as the Countess Almaviva in Mozart's *The Marriage of Figaro* at Boston's Tremont Theatre. By December of that year she was appearing with a touring opera company in New Orleans. It was here that her singing career came to an ungracious end. Either because she had been pushed into soprano roles too uncomfortable for her natural contralto voice, or because she had been singing too strenuously without proper coaching, the early bloom of her voice was gone. The kindest of the New Orleans critics was certainly the one who suggested that she should spare the public and limit herself to non-singing roles. On 23 April 1836 she made her dramatic debut at the St. Charles Theatre in no less a starring role than that of Lady Macbeth. She was an immediate success and her career as America's greatest actress of the century was begun. That it happened to be Shakespeare's birthday was indeed a good omen for her.

Her debut at New York's Bowery Theatre came in September of 1836, and in May of the following year, with an ever-growing entourage of enthusiastic fans to applaud her efforts, she first appeared as Meg Merrilies in *Guy Mannering*. The effect she created as Sir Walter Scott's gypsy hag was from all reports one of the most outstanding characterizations on the nineteenth-century stage. In February of 1845 she made her London debut at the Princess Theatre as Bianca in Milman's *Fazio*. Her reputation grew steadily as she acted in England in *Othello* with Edwin Forrest and in *Macbeth* with William Macready, and she held her own against both these formidable stage personalities. She was not exactly beloved by the latter when the London papers compared Charlotte's "fiery eloquence" to his "measured emotions and frigid mannerisms." She played Romeo there for the first time in 1846. Being not the most feminine of actresses, she reveled in so-called "trouser roles" and took justifiable pride in her acting of Oberon, Cardinal Wolsey, and Hamlet, as well as Juliet's teen-age lover.

In 1849 she returned triumphantly to the United States acclaimed as an international success and hailed as "Our Charlotte." By 15 May 1852 she had decided to retire from the stage at the height of her popularity and acted Meg Merrilies as her "farewell" to New York. She had the good sense, however, to know when to interrupt her "retirement" to alleviate her boredom and accelerate her finances. After only two years of residence in Rome, she was back on the London stage. During the season of 1857 and 1858 she acted again in the United States and, although the country was in the midst of a depression, her box-office intake broke records everywhere she appeared. Then home again to Rome. She became almost a commuter across the Atlantic. She was in the United States in 1860 and 1863, when she aided the American Sanitary Commission by acting in a series of benefits for Civil War relief. A trip in 1868 involved only personal business and no acting. When not traveling, she was at home in Rome where she played host to the leading American and English literati who frequented the Eternal City. She mothered a small tribe of relatives and female protégées and signed her notes to them "Big Mama." In 1870 she returned to the United States for the last time and kept busy on her beloved stage almost until the time of her death. She acted at Booth's Theatre in New York for forty-two nights beginning 25 September 1871, and the engagement brought in an unprecedented $57,000. Late in 1872 she began a career as a reader. Her last stage appearance was as Lady Macbeth at Booth's Theatre on 7 November 1874. As a tribute to America's greatest tragedienne, the curtain was rung down immediately after the famous "Sleepwalking Scene"—exactly as had been done at the farewell of her illustrious English predecessor Sarah Siddons. She died in Boston on 18 February 1876.

Charlotte Cushman, 1816-1876

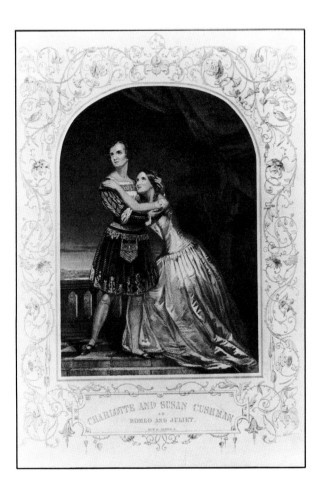

32, 33. *Above*: Charlotte and Susan Cushman as Romeo and Juliet. This engraving, published in London by John Tallis in 1850 or 1851, probably served as the model for a Staffordshire ceramic figure of the two actresses. *Opposite page*: Charlotte Cushman, by an unidentified artist, painted at about the time of her operatic debut in 1835.

34. Charlotte Cushman about 1850. This daguerreotype was made
in the Boston studio of Southworth and Hawes.

VI. Geraldine Farrar by Friedrich August von Kaulbach, 1904.

VII. Ira Aldridge in the title role of Shakespeare's *Othello* by the English painter Henry Perronet Briggs, circa 1826.

VIII. Joseph Jefferson as Peter Pangloss in George Colman Jr.'s *The Heir-at-Law* by John Singer Sargent, 1891.

IX. Edwin Booth as Iago in William Shakespeare's *Othello* by
Thomas Hicks, 1863. This painting is a small version of the life-size
portrait now at The Players in New York City. The original caused
much comment when first exhibited. Hicks depicts the moment
when Iago delivers the line, "This is the night that either makes me,
or foregoes me quite."

X. Julia Marlowe by Irving R. Wiles, 1901.

Jenny Lind was twenty-eight years old when she retired from the operatic stage in May of 1849. She had been the darling of Europe for eleven years, rating ovations and rewards greater than those paid to any previous soprano. Even Queen Victoria herself attended all of Jenny's performances during her farewell engagement in London. She had not, however, given up the concert stage and so, when P. T. Barnum's agent caught up with her in Lubeck, Germany, in January of 1850, she signed a contract to appear in America.

Her debut was prepared with all the masterful showmanship that Barnum could muster, and, as soon as she appeared on the dock at New York on the first Sunday in September, 1850, a wave of mass hysteria began to roll before she had even sung a note. Items of clothing and furniture were named for her, and her likeness appeared in thousands of lithographs and on glass bottles and tobacco labels. Frequently the icon that was circulated was one based upon the beatific image in her 1846 portrait by Eduard Magnus. To begin with, a print of it graced the cover of the program of her first American concert.

To heighten the excitement Barnum hit upon the idea of auctioning off the tickets to the first concert in each city where she would appear. In New York a hatter name Genin—who just happened to be a friend of Barnum—won the first ticket for $225. Providence and Philadelphia buyers were later to shame him by paying $650 and $625, respectively. During rehearsal for her first American concert at New York's Castle Garden on 11 September 1850, Jenny had no sooner begun to sing when she was interrupted by a one-hundred gun salute celebrating the admission of California to the Union. She took it as a good omen. Her debut concert, which opened with the "Casta Diva" from Bellini's *Norma* and ended with a saccharine piece called "Welcome to America," written especially for the occasion by Julius Benedict to a prize-winning text by Bayard Taylor, was notable not only for the artistry of the singing and the applause, but for several innovations in theater management. Barnum, correctly predicting an immense sellout audience, had color-coded the auditorium and the tickets to make seating simpler and had used detachable ticket stubs for the first time. As was so often her practice in Europe, where her piety and generosity endeared her to monarchs and subjects alike, she gave her $10,000 share of the first-night proceeds to charity.

Throughout the rest of her ninety-three-concert tour under Barnum's management, Jenny Lind became even more of a national sensation. Daniel Webster and Henry Wadsworth Longfellow came to pay their respects to her in Boston, and in Washington, where a new hall was being built just for her first appearance there—it was, of course, not finished on time—Millard Fillmore called on her in her quarters. She was not in, so she later graciously returned the call at the White House.

The Philadelphia audience, upholding its reputation as the hardest to please in the nation, gave her a cool reception when she first appeared on stage, but was cheering with as much frenzy as the rest of the nation by the end of the first half of the concert. By the time she had made her grand tour and returned to Philadelphia on 9 May 1851 for her last concert under Barnum management, the wily impresario had pocketed $535,486 in box-office receipts while his "Swedish Nightingale" had personally earned another $176,675.

Leaving Barnum's flamboyant, but lucrative management, she embarked upon a forty-concert tour of her own and found that the American audiences who had adored her for the past eight months were turning fickle. Critics found her new accompanist, Otto Goldschmidt, too formal and too dull, and they began to hint at Jenny's pigheadedness and temperament. The tour was not a complete loss, however, for she married Goldschmidt in Boston on 5 February 1852. Her last American concert was sung at Castle Garden on 24 May 1852, and five days later Mr. and Mrs. Goldschmidt took ship for England.

Jenny Lind, 1820-1887

As Jenny Goldschmidt she concertized until her final performance in Handel's *Messiah* in Düsseldorf in 1866. In 1883, at the request of the Prince of Wales, she became the First Professor of Singing at London's new Royal College of Music. She died in her English country home on 2 November 1887 and was buried, as she had requested, with a shawl given her by Queen Victoria and a patchwork quilt presented to her by children during her American tour.

35, 36, 37. *Left:* An 1850 New York broadside of Bayard Taylor's *Greeting to America.* The head of Jenny Lind is taken from the Eduard Magnus portrait of the famous singer. *Above:* The head of Jenny Lind from the Magnus portrait is pressed into service as a tobacco label, 1850. *Opposite page:* A replica, painted about 1861, of the Eduard Magnus portrait of 1846.

Remembered principally as a playwright, Dion Boucicault was born Dionysius Lardner Boursiquot in Dublin and began his association with the theater as an actor in provincial English playhouses under the name Lee Moreton. His first successful play, *London Assurance*, was produced in 1841. From 1844 until 1848 he was in France, where he met and married a French widow who mysteriously fell from a cliff while they were vacationing in the Alps.

Dion Boucicault came to the United States for the first time in the fall of 1853. He had married the young actress Agnes Robertson in London and joined her in New York, where she made her debut in a musical that he had adapted from an older work. Agnes Robertson's success prompted an American tour during which her husband acted with her. Back in New York, Boucicault began to write and produce the long series of plays which kept him a favorite of American audiences during most of his stage career. *The Poor of New York* was a graphic if overly dramatic comment on the financial crisis of 1857, and *The Octoroon*, first produced in 1859, was so judiciously worded as to win the approbation of both slaveholders and abolitionists. In 1860 Boucicault produced *The Colleen Bawn*, the first of his comedies on an Irish theme. This play, a dramatization of Gerald Griffin's novel, *The Collegians*, was followed by three other plays in the same vein. Together these constitute the greatest monument to Dion Boucicault's abilities. *Arah-na-Pogue* appeared in 1864, *The O'Dowd* in 1873, and the following year the most famous of all, *The Shaughraun*. Boucicault excelled in Irish character roles, and his own plays were his greatest vehicles. By the time of his appearances as Conn in *The Shaughraun*, he had raised the stock comic character of the Irishman to the height of respectability. His popularity in the role prompted the New York sculptor John Rogers, whose interest in the theater was primarily commercial, to model Boucicault in character for production as a plaster parlor ornament. In the spring of 1875 one of the completed statuettes was presented to Boucicault by Irish-American residents of New York as a testimonial of their appreciation for what his writing and acting had done to further the estate of the Irish in America.

Boucicault returned to London from 1862 until 1872, and in 1885 he went to Australia for a short time. His major achievements, however, remained connected with the history of the New York stage. In addition to his writing and acting, he had also instituted the practice of casting a play in New York and sending a completed production on tour. It was a practice that had serious effects on the older tradition of local stock companies. Dion Boucicault appeared on stage for the last time in 1886. Having spent his fortunes almost before he acquired them, he had sunk to the relatively insignificant position of a teacher of acting at the time of his death in New York on 18 September 1890.

38, 39. *Opposite page (left)*: The bronze master model for the plaster figure of Dion Boucicault as Conn with his dog Tatters in *The Shaughraun*. Both the actor and the dog sat for John Rogers in December, 1874. The sculptor's sketchbook contains the actor's measurements and a sketch of the dog. *Opposite page (right)*: Dion Boucicault as seen by the artist Spy (Sir Leslie Ward). The caricature was published in *Vanity Fair*, December 16, 1882.

Dion Boucicault, 1822-1890

THE SHAUGHRAUN AND "TATTERS"

The iconography of the early days of the classical ballet in the United States was entrusted largely to the lithographers of the period. On sheet music covers and in single sheet prints the dancers were frozen in motion for the newly adoring public. Some of the likenesses of the native talent were awkward, but original creations. Images of the visiting Europeans were often pirated from European prints that had preceded their arrivals. In one case, at least, an Italian artist honored an American *danseuse* who went on to fame across the Atlantic.

As early as age eleven Mary Ann Lee was playing various children's roles on the Philadelphia stage, but she made her official debut as a dancer on 30 December 1837 as Fatima in *The Maid of Cashmere* when she was twelve or thirteen. Her rival in the small company of the Chestnut Street Theatre was twelve-year-old Augusta Maywood, who was later to go on to fame in Europe. In September of the following year Mary Ann transferred her allegiance to the Walnut Street Theatre where she danced the new ballet, *The Lily Queen*, produced especially for her. Between dances she acted Albert in support of Edwin Forrest's William Tell. In April of 1838 Mary Ann's success as Zoloe in the ballet *La Bayadere* led to her engagement by the Bowery Theatre in New York where she made her debut on June 12 in the same work. There on 8 July she danced the Cachucha for President Martin Van Buren. She appeared at P. T. Barnum's Vauxhall Gardens and, to further her career, studied with Fanny Elssler's partner James Sylvain while the famed Viennese prima ballerina was appearing at the Park Theatre. To the delight of the nationalists in her audience, she dared dance the Cachucha at Vauxhall while Elssler was performing it at the Park.

After a tour of the United States, which took her as far afield as New Orleans and Mobile, she went off to Paris from November of 1844 until September of 1845 to study with the staff of the ballet at the Opéra. Her progress in her studies was eagerly followed by American fans of ballet, and she made a triumphant second debut in *La Jolie Fille du Grand* at Philadelphia's Arch Street Theatre on 24 November 1845. One month later she began a tour with a company she had newly organized around herself, and in Boston on 1 January 1846, with George Washington Smith as her Albrecht, she performed the first American production of the now venerable and perennial favorite *Giselle*. We have no review of that premiere, but of a performance at the Park Theatre on 14 April 1846, the correspondent of the *New York Herald* commented: ". . . Miss Lee enacted Giselle with beauty, charm, elegance and grace that cannot be described, and we will not attempt it . . . ." What was the pinnacle of her career became the climax, for during her tour of 1846-1847 her health began to fail and she was obliged to dance her farewell performance on the stage of the Arch Street Theatre on 18 June 1847.

None but the most vehement of her followers would have claimed she was the equal of Fanny Elssler and the other noted European dancers who were exhibiting their virtuosity to American audiences at that time. She was admired everywhere, however, as the best American ballerina of her time, and one whose charming stage personality and presence drew sympathetic and enthusiastic audiences. What height of greatness she might have achieved as a dancer these audiences would never know—for she was forced to retire at age twenty-four. She died in 1899.

Mary Ann Lee, 1823-1899

40. Mary Ann Lee dancing *La Smolenska* on a cover to sheet music published in Boston by William Oates, 1842.

Although she was born Augusta Williams, it was under the family name of her actor-manager stepfather, Robert Campbell Maywood, that America's first internationally famous dancer achieved professional renown. After instruction by the Philadelphia dancing teachers Madame and Monsieur Paul Hazard, Augusta Maywood made her debut in that city's Chestnut Street Theatre on 30 December 1837, dancing the role of Zelica in *The Maid of Cashmere*. Ably promoted by her stepfather—who at this point was manager of the theatre—she became an overnight sensation, not only in her home city, but also in New York where she made her Park Theatre debut on 12 February 1838.

Sometime later, "La Petite Augusta," as she was called on playbills and in the press, sailed for France to complete her dance education with Jean Coralli in the ballet school of the Paris Opera. On 11 November 1839 she made her Opéra debut dancing a pas de deux with Charles Mabille in the first act of her teacher's ballet *Le Diable boiteux*. The critics received her with great praise, and she was engaged by the Opéra for a year at a salry of 3,000 francs. Her career in Paris ended when she eloped with Charles Mabille almost exactly one year from the date of her debut. The newly married couple danced together in France for several years and then during the season of 1843-1844 appeared at the Theatro de São Carlos in Lisbon.

In 1845 Augusta deserted her husband and resumed dancing under her own name. She was never to return to Paris but went on to great fame in other European dance capitals. In 1845 she was declared prima ballerina at Vienna's Hofburgoperntheater where she was one of the first to demand, and achieve, equal billing with famous guest artists. In 1848 she was engaged for the first time by Milan's Teatro de la Scala. With the great Austrian ballerina Fanny Elssler, she alternated dancing the lead role in the premiere performances of Jules Perrot's great ballet *Faust* and also shared, as incongruous as it seems, the title of "prima ballerina e prima mima assoluta."

About this time she became one of the first dancers to organize and travel with a semi-permanent company, joining with Giuseppe and Giovanni Battista Lasina to create a notable company that toured Italy during one of that country's great eras of dance. Except for one return engagement in Vienna in 1854, Augusta Maywood devoted the remainder of her career to dancing in Italy. When one reads the comments that Italian journalists made about her, ("queen of the air," "new Terpsichore," "incomparable both as mime and dancer"), there is no doubt of her celebrity. She appeared in works by Italy's leading choreographers, one of the most interesting—from an American point of view—Giuseppe Rota's *I Bianchi ed i negri*, which premiered in Milan on 10 November 1853. One year after its first publication in Italian, Harriet Beecher Stowe's *Uncle Tom's Cabin* was danced as a ballet in Milan, anticipating the quaint version in *The King and I* by a century. Although records are incomplete, it is presumed that Augusta Maywood danced Little Eva.

In 1856 she danced for the first time Filippo Termanini's *Rita Gauthier*, a role that became associated particularly with her and, although a trifle, one she danced frequently until the end of her career, alternating it with masterpieces such as Perrot's *Faust* and *Esmeralda*. She danced for the last time in 1859 and opened a school of ballet in Vienna. Her death occurred from smallpox in what is now the city of Lvov, Poland, on 3 November 1876.

Augusta Maywood, 1825-1876

41. Augusta Maywood in the title role of the ballet *Rita Gauthier*. This rare lithograph was drawn by A. Bedetti and was printed in Ancona, Italy, by the Pieroni firm in 1856.

Born in the tiny village of Blakes, Ireland, on 14 November 1832, John McCullough was an illiterate youth when he came to Philadelphia in 1847. While teaching himself to read, he discovered Shakespeare and soon joined an amateur theatrical group. After elocution lessons with Lemuel White, Edwin Forrest's teacher, he made his professional debut at the Arch Street Theatre on 15 August 1857. His first role was that of Thomas in *The Belle's Stratagem*. After spending the season 1860-1861 with Boston's Howard Athenaeum, he was chosen by Edwin Forrest to be second actor in the American tragedian's company.

In physique and stage manner he was like Forrest and, after five years of acting with him, the younger actor was criticized as being imitative. In 1866 McCullough left Forrest's company during a California tour and remained in San Francisco. In 1869 he was co-manager of that city's new California Theatre with Lawrence Barrett, and, at the latter's withdrawal in 1870, he became the sole manager and chief actor at that house for the next five years. McCullough began a series of national tours in 1873 and then returned to the East Coast for further acting lessons. New York critics who had once found fault with his unsubtle and boisterous acting now praised him.

In the period from 1877 to 1883 he was at his peak as an actor of noble characters—Virginius, Brutus, Julius Ceasar, and Lear—and was favorably received. He was at his best in moments of rage, pathos, or passionate outbursts. He said that he experienced in actuality the emotions of the characters he was playing. Fellow actors often saw him shaking and weeping at the conclusion of a strong scene.

About 1883 his health began to decline and he took a long vacation, returning to the stage in the autumn of 1884. During a performance of Robert Montgomery Bird's *The Gladiator* at McVicker's Theatre in Chicago on 29 September, he suffered a mental and physical breakdown and had to be helped from the stage. From 27 June to 25 October of 1885 he was confined to a New York sanitarium. Taken home to Philadelphia, he died there on 8 November 1885.

John McCullough, 1832-1885

42. John McCullough in the title role of James Sheridan Knowles's *Virginius*. The portrait was done posthumously by Eastman Johnson in 1892 and was based on a photograph.

Joseph Jefferson was the third of his name to appear on the American stage. His actor grandfather had emigrated from England in 1795, and his father was a traveling player and painter. Joseph was born in Philadelphia on 20 February 1829 and made his acting debut in Washington at age four, when, performing with Thomas "Jim Crow" Rice, he appeared as a miniature replica of the famous blackface comedian. In 1837 he went with his family on a tour of the West and South. His father died during the tour, and Joseph at age thirteen became the head of the family. In 1846, during the Mexican War, he even followed the United States Army across the border with the hopes of financial reward for his talents. By 1849 he had returned to New York where he joined the company at Chanfrau's National Theatre. In 1853 he was actor and stage manager in Baltimore, and in 1856 he made a trip to England and the Continent to observe the acting there as an aid to improving his own technique.

Returning to New York he was engaged by Laura Keene at her theater and made his first big hit on 31 August 1857 when he acted Dr. Pangloss in George Colman's *The Heir-at-Law*. Upon the death of his wife in 1861, he left the United States and spent four years performing in Australia and Tasmania. In 1865 he returned to New York and left almost immediately for London where he and Dion Boucicault prepared for a new stage version of Washington Irving's *Rip Van Winkle*. The greatness of his characterization of the title role was recognized immediately by the British public when he first performed the role at London's Adelphi Theatre on 4 September 1865, and, when they saw him as Rip for the first time almost exactly a year later, on 3 September 1866, New Yorkers echoed the cheers of their cousins across the Atlantic. Joe Jefferson, as he was fondly called by his adoring American public, became a national institution as Rip Van Winkle. For almost forty years, he toured the country annually in the role and put away the costumes for almost all of his characters, retaining only those for Dr. Pangloss and one or two others.

He staged a revival of Richard Brinsley Sheridan's *The Rivals* with himself as Bob Acres at Philadelphia's Arch Street Theatre in 1880 and added this role to the select few he offered his public. Rip Van Winkle, of course, was his most popular role, and, though he was proud and serious about his art, he could laugh at himself and refer to the endless performances as "the theatrical swindle." In 1893, upon the death of Edwin Booth, The Players acknowledged his preeminence among American actors by electing him the second president of the organization. After seventy-one years on stage, he last acted at Paterson, New Jersey, on 7 May 1904 as Caleb Plummer and Mr. Golightly in a double bill of *The Cricket on the Hearth* and *Lend Me Five Shillings*. He died at his home in Palm Beach, Florida, on 23 April 1905.

43. *Opposite page*: Joseph Jefferson as Peter Pangloss in George Colman Jr.'s *The Heir-at-Law*, by John Singer Sargent, 1891. This portrait appears in color on p. 70.

Joseph Jefferson, 1829-1905

44, 45. *Left*: Joseph Jefferson and an unidentified actor in *The Rivals*. The photograph is thought to have been made in 1898. *Below*: Jefferson in the first act of his adaptation of Washington Irving's *Rip Van Winkle*, "Rip Van Winkle at Home." The final two "acts" of John Rogers's plaster parlor figures appear on the following page.

46, 47. Acts 2 and 3, "Rip Van Winkle on the Mountain" and "Rip Van Winkle Returns." These bronzes are the master models for the plaster parlor figures marketed by John Rogers. Joseph Jefferson actually posed for the artist, and Rogers stated that fact in his sales catalogues.

When his fourth son was born near Bel Air, Maryland, on 13 November 1833, Junius Brutus Booth named the child Edwin after his friend Edwin Forrest. The boy accompanied his father on theatrical tours from a very early date, and his filial responsibilities as a result of his father's increasingly erratic behavior forced on him a grave and melancholy temperament that was never to leave him. On 10 September 1849, young Edwin made his first appearance on stage at the Boston Museum as Tressel in *Richard III*. Two years later he made his debut in a major role when he had to assume the title role in the same work upon his father's indisposition. Edwin accompanied his father and brother Junius Brutus, Jr., to California in 1852. The elder Booth left California sometime later and died on the trip home. Edwin, now on his own, acted for a while in California and Nevada and in 1854 embarked upon a tour of Australia, where, in Sydney, he acted Shylock for the first time.

On the return trip home he stopped for two months in Honolulu, where he produced *Richard III* in the presence of King Kamehameha IV. Booth appeared with increasing popularity in San Francisco and Sacramento, and, when he returned to the East Coast, he was an experienced and accomplished actor, especially skillful in tragic and highly dramatic roles. He made a spectacular success in Boston in April of 1857 as Sir Giles Overreach in *The Iron Chest* and later in the same year won the approbation of New York audiences for performances in *Richard III* and *Othello*. His Iago in the latter play was especially admired. His tour in England in 1861 was moderately successful.

For the next three years he was seen principally at the Winter Garden Theatre in New York, which for a while he managed. It was there in 1864 that he gave his unprecedented 100-night run of *Hamlet*, a role in which he was particularly successful since it fitted his own temperament so well. His melancholy was compounded when his younger brother, John Wilkes Booth, assassinated Abraham Lincoln in Washington on that dreadfully misnamed Good Friday in 1865. Although threats had been made on Edwin's life as a result of the murder, he returned to the stage and to generally appreciative audiences at the Winter Garden on 3 January 1866.

The theater burned in March of the following year and he immediately planned a building to replace it. Booth's Theatre opened on 3 February 1869, and, from then until the season of 1873-1874, when the economic panic in the country forced Booth into bankruptcy, it was the scene of the most notable theatricals that this country had known. Upon Edwin Forrest's death late in 1872, Booth was acknowledged as America's leading actor. In 1878 he had published the annotated text of fifteen of his most frequently performed productions under the title *Edwin Booth's Prompt Book*. In 1881 he appeared at London's Princess Theatre for a 119-night engagement and shortly after played at the Lyceum with Henry Irving, alternating with him the roles of Othello and Iago.

From 1887 he played in America principally with Lawrence Barrett and Helena Modjeska and in 1888 founded The Players in a house he had purchased on Gramercy Park in New York. Almost a century later, the famous club still occupies Booth's house. His farewell from the stage was as Hamlet at the Brooklyn Academy of Music on 4 April 1891. It was a role he had made his own. All performances in America were henceforth to be judged by it. He died 7 June 1893.

Surely no other actor of the American stage has been so often honored by painters and sculptors as Edwin Booth. Hanging on the walls of The Players alone there are enough likenesses by noteworthy painters and sculptors to fill a small gallery.

Edwin Booth, 1833-1893

48. John Wilkes Booth, Edwin Booth, and Junius Brutus Booth, Jr., in Roman costume. The photograph is thought to have been made about the time that the three brothers acted together in Shakespeare's *Julius Caesar* at New York's Winter Garden Theatre, November 25, 1864.

49. Edwin Booth in the title role of Shakespeare's *Hamlet*, by William Wallace Scott, 1870. The artist has very carefully rendered the details of the set in use by Booth at that time. A color portrait of Booth as Iago appears on p. 71.

50. Edwin Booth as the pensive scholar who contemplated the portraits of the great actors of the past. This is a nineteenth-century engraving after an unlocated portrait from life.

51. Edwin Booth and his daughter Edwina.

The son of a German opera-singer mother and an English wine-merchant father, Richard Mansfield was born in Germany on 24 May 1854 and came to America with his mother in 1872. In Boston, where they settled, he joined an amateur theatrics group and appeared on stage for the first time early in 1876. He wanted to be a painter and in 1877 returned to London, where he soon learned that his chosen profession would not be lucrative. He began giving entertainments in private homes and music halls and toured for a while as Sir Joseph Porter in Gilbert and Sullivan's operetta *H. M. S. Pinafore*.

He returned to the United States in April of 1882 and made his first really professional appearance on an American stage at New York's Standard Theatre as Dromez in the operetta *Les Manteaux Noirs* on 27 September. He played stock and operetta for three years and in September of 1885, after a very short return trip to London, he was again in New York supporting Minnie Maddern in *In Spite of All*. His first real success was in the title role of Archibald C. Gunter's *Prince Karl*, which he first acted in Boston on 5 April 1886. From there the play went to New York and then on tour for exactly one year.

On 9 May 1887 Mansfield performed for the first time in the dual roles of Dr. Jekyll and Mr. Hyde in the play by Thomas Russell Sullivan. Throughout his career his audiences were never to tire of watching his evidently spectacular onstage transformation from one character to another. In August of 1888 he took the play to London and while there acted Shakespeare for the first time. The role was Richard III and it was to remain one of his most popular.

On 19 May 1890 at New York's Madison Square Theatre he added Clyde Fitch's *Beau Brummel* to his growing repertoire, and in 1893 he acted Shylock for the first time. On 17 September 1894 he produced *Arms and the Man* at the Herald Square Theatre. It was the first production of a George Bernard Shaw play that America had seen, and although it was not exactly an overwhelming success—it lasted sixteen performances—Mansfield chose it to open his management of the Garrick Theatre in April of 1895. He also produced the second Shaw play in America—*The Devil's Disciple* —which opened in Albany on 1 October 1897. From 1900 to 1906 he produced and acted in a repertoire that included not only his favored characterizations, but Shakespeare's *Henry V* and *Julius Caesar*, Booth Tarkington's *Monsieur Beaucaire*, and the first performance in this country of Henrik Ibsen's *Peer Gynt*.

His style was highly individual, and he was as committed to scrupulous preparation of a production as was his contemporary Mrs. Fiske, but sadly lacked her offstage personality and her consideration for subordinates. His outbursts of temperament were legend in his profession long before his death. He fell ill after acting a double bill in New York on 23 March 1907 and died at his home in New London, Connecticut, on 23 August of that year. When he died, there were those who saw the passing of an era, an era of the "grand style" and of American repertory theater.

Richard Mansfield, 1854-1907

52. Richard Mansfield as Beau Brummel, by Orlando Rouland, 1907.

The son and grandson of Universalist ministers, Otis Skinner was born in Cambridge, Massachusetts, on 28 June 1858. Disdaining to follow the family calling, he began his theatrical career with the acting company of the Philadelphia Museum on 30 October 1877 as Jim, an old Negro, in Phillip Stoner's *Woodleigh*. In his first season of apprenticeship he played ninety-two different characters.

Although his first New York appearance was made supporting John McCullough in *Coriolanus*, he considered his real debut in that city his appearance as Maclow in *Enchantment*, first produced at Niblo's Gardens on 4 September 1879. He supported Edwin Booth and Lawrence Barrett for a while and for three years was a member of Augustin Daly's company. In 1894 he produced and starred in what was to be the first romantic role favored by his public, *His Grace de Grammont* by Clyde Fitch. Physically and temperamentally endowed as an ideal romantic hero, Otis Skinner remained popular with his audiences by the happy coincidence of his greatest roles. In 1907 Broadway saw him in the comic part of Colonel Phillipe Bridau in *The Honor of the Family*, and he achieved his greatest fame in the role of Hajj in *Kismet* by Edward Knoblock. After playing the role for three years in New York and on tour, he made a silent film version of the play and still later a sound version.

His career onstage lasted fifty-eight years and encompassed 325 parts. He outlived Edwin Booth by fifty years and was therefore one of the last of the American actors trained in the traditions of the nineteenth century, traditions of versatility and the grand manner. His style was at odds with the major developments in the theater in the first years of this century, and his undiminished popularity until the time of his retirement must be taken as a tribute to his talents. His last appearance was as Uncle Tom in a 1933 revival of Mrs. Stowe's famous melodrama. He died in New York on 4 January 1942.

Otis Skinner, 1858-1942

53. *Opposite page*: James Montgomery Flagg's drawing of Otis
Skinner, autographed for a fan by the actor.

54. *Above*: Otis Skinner as Colonel Bridau in *The Honor of the
Family*, by George Luks, 1919.

It's a long way from Fullersburg, Illinois, to Paris, France. Loïe Fuller made the trip with a certain verve that would be hard to exceed. At age four she made her debut with a stock company in Chicago. Impersonations of little boys became her specialty. She toured with Buffalo Bill's Wild West Company and sang at least one performance of grand opera at Hooley's Opera House in Chicago. The stages of both vaudeville and legitimate theater exposed her talent to public view. After a short run in London in a trifle entitled *Caprice*, she returned to New York where, in 1891, she evolved the "Serpentine Dance" which was to bring her fame in both Europe and America. As she danced, she manipulated the folds of a long skirt about her in constantly changing billows. She became enamored with light, and, by the time she had reached Paris in 1892—by way of short engagements with a German theater and a French traveling circus—she had conceived such start-ling innovations in the lighting of her act that she was signed by the Folies-Bergèere. She considered herself "an instrument of light" and invented and named dances that were inspired by colors and by sensations of light. In her "Fire Dance" she performed on a sheet of glass lighted from below in an effort to capture the effects of flame and smoke. It was this dance that inspired a Toulouse-Lautrec lithograph. Loïe Fuller's dancing was everything that the lovers of the then blossoming Art Nouveau style wanted from a work of art. It had color, sinuous line, and real movement. Instantly, she was the idol of Paris.

In 1896 she returned to New York for a short engagement at Koster and Bial's Music Hall and en-thralled that city's audiences as she had those in the French capital. Her weekly salary was reputed to be twice that of the ever-popular Lillian Russell.

Back in France she picnicked with Auguste Rodin, was introduced to the French Astronomical Society by Camille Flammarion, the celebrated astronomer, was depicted on posters by Jules Cheret and other leading artists of the genre, and she became the inspiration for a bronze lamp by Raoul Larche. She was, as well, the inspiration for a ceramic vase by R. Jeandelle and bronzes by Charles Louchet, Clara Pfeffer, Theodore Riviere, and Rupert Carabin. In short, she became one of the major motifs of Art Nouveau.

Loïe Fuller's studies of light became quite serious, and she constantly improved and elaborated upon her stage effects. One of her dances, the "Fire Dance" already mentioned, required the ser-vices of fourteen electricians. She became a friend of Pierre and Marie Curie, whose discovery of radium seemed to Loïe the source of a very special lighting effect she might use in her act. In her con-stant search for more impressive lighting effects, she maintained a laboratory with sometimes as many as six employees working on experiments with "fluorescent salts." She once seared some of her hair and was evicted from her quarters when an experiment she was conducting blew up in her face. A troupe which she gathered about her and which she presented in concert included for a while the young Isadora Duncan. Her band of comely young "muses," as she called them, appeared with her in a "Ballet of Light." During the First World War she traveled back and forth between France and America arranging entertainments for servicemen and campaigning for wartime charities.

As early as 1905 she made motion pictures in the Paris studios of the Pathée company. Her last professional performance, in 1927, was in a "Shadow Ballet" which utilized silhouette effects sug-gested to her by the developments in cinema technique. In her never-ending efforts to create new stage lighting lies her great contribution to stagecraft. Her contributions to choreography, if there were any, have paled aside her ability to create an effect. She summed up her position herself when she said, "I suppose I am the only person who is known as a dancer but who has a personal preference for Science."

Loïe Fuller, 1862-1928

55. Gilded metal electric lamp designed in the shape of Loïe Fuller, by Raoul Larche, about 1900.

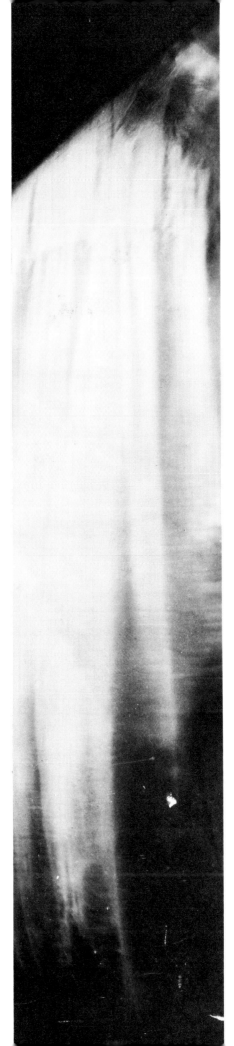

56, 57. *Opposite page:* The real Loïe Fuller swishing her veils, a photograph by Benjamin J. Falk, 1901. *Above:* Loïe Fuller in her *Fire Dance,* a hand-colored lithograph by Henri Toulouse-Lautrec, 1893.

The daughter of theatrical parents, Maria August Davey was born in New Orleans on 19 December 1865. She is said to have made her stage debut in Little Rock, Arkansas, at the age of three using the name "Little Minnie Maddern." She was seen in New York for the first time in 1870 in two different roles, one of them Little Eva in *Uncle Tom's Cabin*. By the time she made her real professional debut at the Park Theatre in May 1882, she had had experience in a wide range of theatrics. In 1884 she was very successful in a musical called *Caprice*. On 19 May 1890 she married Harrison Grey Fiske, editor of the *New York Dramatic Mirror*, and briefly retired from the stage. She returned again in 1894 as "the tragedienne Mrs. Fiske" in the title role of her husband's *Hester Crewe*.

With *Hester Crewe*, a naturalistic drama, both playwright and actress attempted to break away from the histrionic traditions of the nineteenth century. After long years of practice and experience, she evolved a personal style which made her a pioneer of the American stage. She emphasized a truthfulness and true-to-life portrayal of her characters, and she strove for a production in which the performers and stage effects were all subordinate to the overall aim of the author. It would be years before the rest of her profession and the public caught up with her ideals. Realizing that all in life was not proverbial sweetness and light, she achieved great success in portrayals of immoral and unsavory women in such plays as Lorrimer Stoddard's *Tess of the D'Ubervilles* (1897) and Langdon Mitchell's *Becky Sharp* (1899), based respectively on novels by Hardy and Thackeray.

Most of her history-making productions were staged between 1901 and 1907 at the Manhattan Theatre, which her husband had bought for her when the Klaw and Erlanger syndicate evicted her from the Fifth Avenue Theatre at the height of her success in *Becky Sharp*. A champion of Henrik Ibsen in a day when American cirtics and playgoers thought him immoral and subversive, she first played Noral in his *A Doll's House* at a benefit in 1894 and produced *Hedda Gabler* and *Rosmershold* at her own theater in 1903 and 1907. Against the fulminations of critics and clergymen alike, she played the latter Ibsen work for an unprecedented 199 performances at a profit. She acted Mrs. Alving in her fifth Ibsen production, *Ghosts*, which toured the country in 1927.

During the latter part of her career she acted mainly in lighter comedy, and one of her last roles was as Beatrice in *Much Ado about Nothing*, the first Shakespeare she had played since her childhood. She declared acting to be a science and she devoted her entire life to it. Outside of the theater her only interest was the prevention of cruelty to animals and the wanton slaying of animals and birds for fur and feathers. During her last years she revived some of her earlier successes and took them on the road. Illness forced her to cancel her tour early in 1932 and she died at her Hollis, Long Island, home on 15 February of that year.

60. *Opposite page*: Minnie Maddern Fiske looking very much like one of Ibsen's heroines, by M. Colin, 1893.

Minnie Maddern Fiske, 1865-1932

Carmencita was one of the first "ethnic" dancers to appear in the United States. She was not an immediate success when she first appeared at Niblo's Garden in New York, but in the spring of 1890, while dancing nightly at Koster and Bial's Music Hall, she became one of the most popular theatrical attractions in the city. Readers of the theatrical columns were told that she lived on Amontillado sherry and fruit and were treated to speculation that she had heart disease and to delightfully frank descriptions of their heroine at home. Newspaper gossip to the contrary, she had a sound heart, but she was a disappointment to those who saw her in her unguarded moments off-stage. A less than exotic flower, she was a hard worker who danced nightly at the music halls, tutored matinee dancing classes in Madison Avenue mansions, and appeared in private concerts for select groups in artists' studios.

The thought of seeing the Spanish dancer in so terribly chic and romantic an atmosphere as a studio so excited millionairess Isabella Stewart Gardner that she made a special trip from Boston for a command performance in the studio of William Merritt Chase. The co-host was John Singer Sargent. At the end of a particularly rousing dance, delighted guests threw flowers and jewelry. One of the ladies reflected upon her overemotional response and the next day asked that her trinket be returned. Carmencita, bless her heart, refused.

Chase memorialized the event with a gold bracelet rolling across the floor in his large painting of the dancer. Sargent also painted her in the winter of 1890, and his portrait went into the French national collections in Paris.

The true measure of Carmencita's success in America was in the number of imitators who came after her. Because she was first, or because she was so good, they never quite measured up.

61. *Opposite page:* Carmencita, by William Merritt Chase, 1890.

Carmencita (Carmen Dauset), 1868-?

After a short career as a child actress on the West Coast, Maude Adams came to New York and made her first professional appearance in that city in September of 1888. She acted with E. H. Sothern and was leading lady to John Drew for five years before becoming a star in her own right. On 27 September 1897 she appeared at the Empire Theatre for the first time as Lady Babbie in James Barrie's *The Little Minister.* An unidentified reviewer has left us an honest and engaging description of her appearance in her first starring role: "Miss Adams is a fascinating gypsy, with queer little gestures and an odd tiptoe walk that is like no gait ever affected by a sane human creature, but somehow seems to fit the part . . . . Her speech is eerie—but not too eerie." Sensing that Adams would color all her characters with her own personality, the critic Alan Dale wrote shortly after her opening that "Any role that is bijou, archly feminine, girlishly effervescent and plaintive will suit this elf-actress. Let her avoid the Juliets and the Rosalinds and the Fedoras and the Camilles. Let her listen to those who know better than she does, and Miss Adams will remain with us, and her art will grow even more subtle."

Either Dale was a prophet or Maude Adams listened to advice. She avoided all roles that did not feature youthful, good, and optimistic characters, and she excelled in the realm of the sweetly sentimental. On 6 November 1905 she opened again at the Empire and again in a play by Barrie. It was *Peter Pan*—the most favored and memorable role for both the actress and her enchanted audiences. Miss Adams valued her privacy, and, even though she became wealthy and famous as the greatest box-office attraction of her time, she never gave press interviews. Even so, the press was kind, and most of what appeared about her in magazines and newspapers extolled her humility and hominess.

In 1918 she retired from the stage and spent some time experimenting with stage lighting. She returned to acting in 1931, playing Portia to Otis Skinner's Shylock in an ill-fated production of *The Merchant of Venice* that never made it to Broadway; she toured summer theaters in a small part in *Twelfth Night* in 1934. In 1937 she joined the faculty of Stephens College, Columbia, Missouri, as professor of dramatic arts. She died at Tannersville, New York, on 17 July 1953.

Maude Adams, 1872-1953

62, 63. *Left*: Maude Adams as Lady Babbie in James Barrie's *The Little Minister*, by Howard Chandler Christy, 1899. *Above*: The actress as Joan of Arc, by Alphonse Mucha, 1909.

For thousands, though they may never have heard his voice on records, the name of the tenor Enrico Caruso evokes the grandness of opera. His career in this country was almost exclusively associated with the Metropolitan Opera. From a short time after his debut there as the Duke of Mantua in Verdi's *Rigoletto* on 23 November 1903 until his 607th performance—and his last—at that house on 24 December 1920 as Eleazar in Jacques Halévy's *La Juive*, he was one of the most important singers on the company roster.

With his powerful voice, bolstered by the enthusiasm of the growing Italian population of New York, he effected a pronounced change upon the repertory which until that time had been top-heavy with Germanic works. Verdi's *Aïda* and Leoncavallo's *I Pagliacci* became, because of his presence in lead roles, audience favorites. Under the baton of Arturo Toscanini from 1908 until 1915, he aided the establishment of the operas of Puccini. In that composer's *La Faniculla del West*, based on a David Belasco play, he created the role of cowboy Dick Johnson at the opera's Metropolitan Opera world premiere on 10 December 1910.

Shortly after his New York debut, he made his first recording for the Victor Talking Machine Company. In an era when some of his fellow singers mistrusted the respectability of the phonograph and recorded under aliases, his open endorsement helped greatly to promote the infant industry. His last recordings, made three months before his final stage performance, includes that which he himself considered his finest: the aria "Rachel, quand du Seigneur," from Halévy's *La Juive*. Caruso had the unprecedented honor of being part of the opening night cast for sixteen of his seventeen years with the Metropolitan Opera. Because he was a most honest critic of his own performances, the endorsement of his paycheck stubs often included a one word appraisal of that evening's performance. They range from "Not so good" to "Magnificent."

In ill health from pleurisy, he left the stage at the end of 1920 and returned to his native Italy. He died at Naples, 9:05 a.m. on the morning of 2 August 1921. The following day, an article by W. J. Henderson in the New York *Sun* became a most accurate and eloquent eulogy:

> In sincerity, in fervor, in devotion to his art, he was the peer of any opera singer in history . . . . He was an indifferent actor and a supreme singer when he came here. He finished his career a singer less flawless, but an operatic interpreter who commanded the respect and sympathy of the severest critics, even when they could not credit him with a triumphant success.

64. *Opposite:* Enrico Caruso as Eleazar in Jacques Halévy's *La Juive*, by Benjamin Kalman, undated.

Enrico Caruso, 1873-1921

65. *Above:* The golden-voiced tenor cast in silver by the Italian sculptor Filippo Cifariello, 1910.

66. *Opposite page:* Enrico Caruso as the Duke of Mantua in Verdi's *Rigoletto*, the role of his debut at the Metropolitan Opera. This photograph was made in New York by Aime Dupont in 1908.

Feodor Chaliapin made his operatic debut at age seventeen with a provincial opera company in his native Russia. In 1901, after having acquired something of a reputation for himself in Moscow as a singing actor, he sang outside of Russia for the first time. He first appeared in New York at the Metropolitan Opera on 20 November 1907 in the title role of Arrigo Boito's *Mefistofele*. So rattled was Henry Krehbiel, the critic of the *New York Tribune*, by Chaliapin's acting and costuming of the role, that he never once mentioned the singer's voice. Cultured New York was more than slightly overcome by what it considered the crudeness and carnality of Chaliapin's handling of the devilish role. In defense of New York it must be said that not that city alone found fault with the Russian singer's characterization in this as well as in other Italian and French operas. However masterful the characterizations might have been, they were incompatible with Victorian tradition and therefore not immediately acceptable.

In the opera of his homeland, however, it was a different matter, and he became truly worthy of being the first Russian singer to win international fame when he appeared as the guilty, soul-tormented hero of Modest Mussorgsky's *Boris Godunov*. New York first heard him in this role on 9 December 1921. Henry Krehbiel's review of this performance was filled with superlatives: "Centenarians with memories stored away with recollections of Kean, Macready, and Forrest (if there be any such alive) might have attended a performance of Boris Godounoff [sic] at the Metropolitan Opera House last night and felt such swelling of the heart as they experienced when tragedy was at its prime in New York . . . . Last night nobility of acting was paired with a beautiful nobility of voice and vocal style." He remained with the Metropolitan through the season of 1928-1929, his last performance with the company being that of Mephistopheles in Gounod's *Faust* on 20 March 1929.

His was an irrepressible personality. He defied the Met management's ban on encores when he thought his public expected them, and, when singing in concert halls, he made up his program as he went along. No programs were given out at his recitals. The audience had to purchase books which contained the texts of all the songs in his repertoire, and he announced his selections as he made them. Self-exiled from Russia, he died in Paris on 12 April 1938.

The singer's son, Boris Chaliapin, frequently stood in the wings while his father performed and did sketches of him in all of his greatest roles. He also painted him in street clothes. The most appropriately grand of his portraits, however, is the twice life-size polychromed plaster bust here reproduced.

Feodor Chaliapin, 1873-1938

67. Feodor Chaliapin in the title role of Modest Mussorgsky's *Boris Godunov*, by Boris Chaliapin. The bust is of polychromed plaster studded with artificial jewels and is twice life size.

Born in Vienna on 2 February 1875, Fritz Kreisler graduated from the Vienna Conservatory at age ten and four years later made his first concert tour of the United States in the company of the pianist Moritz Rosenthal. Their first concert was played in Boston on 9 November 1888. Returning to Europe, Kreisler temporarily gave up his music for the study of medicine in Vienna, art in Paris, and a commission in an Austrian army regiment. Resigning his commission after about a year in uniform, he returned to the study of the violin.

His debut as a violin soloist took place in Berlin in the spring of 1899. Tours of the United States followed between 1901 and 1903, and it was here that he was first acclaimed as a great violinist. With the advent of World War I, the violinist was recalled into the Austrian army, but his second tour of military duty was of very short duration. Three months after his call he was wounded and discharged. He returned to the United States to raise money for his native country through his playing. When the United States entered the war against Austria, he retired from the concert stage but remained in this country.

His return to the concert stage in New York in 1919 was the cause of great joy among his following. His playing was at its finest at about this time, and much of his music was preserved on phonograph records; between 1916 and 1946 he made over 200. On records and in his concerts he frequently played little pieces which he announced as transcriptions of works by the master composers of the eighteenth and nineteenth centuries. In 1935 he brought down on himself the scorn and condemnation of many critics when he announced that he had written most of the compositions himself. His public, not being as narrow-minded as the professional critics, saw this revelation as insufficient reason to desert their favorite. The audiences that filled every concert hall where he appeared zealously applauded both his lilting virtuoso technique and the delightful short compositions which one of the kinder critics called "transfigured salon music."

Fritz Kreisler became a French citizen in 1938 when Germany annexed Austria. When the Nazi army invaded France, he came permanently to America and became a citizen in 1943. He retired from the concert stage in 1950 and died in New York on 29 January 1962.

Fritz Kreisler, 1875-1962

68. Fritz Kreisler in concert, by Boris Chaliapin, 1943.

"A thunder of applause swept through the house. Many people leaped to their feet. Men shouted 'Bravo!' and women waved their handkerchiefs. Pianists of repute were moved almost to tears. Some wiped the moisture from their eyes." The critic was W. J. Henderson of *The New York Times*, and the occasion, the American debut at the Metropolitan Opera House, 29 November 1887, of the eleven-year-old Polish pianist Josef Casimir Hofmann. Born of musical parents in Cracow on 20 January 1876, he had as early as age seven played the first movement of the Beethoven first piano concerto in public concert. Young Josef had already toured in Germany, Scandinavia, and Holland before coming to America. His announced tour of eighty performances in the United States was cut short when the Society for the Prevention of Cruelty to Children protested the exploitation of one so young, and he was taken back to Europe.

There further studies ensued, and eventually, when he was sixteen, he became a pupil of Anton Rubinstein. He appeared again in the United States in 1898 a fully matured artist, many of his critics conceding that no pianist since his venerable teacher had exhibited such consummate command of his instrument. Under the pseudonym Michel Dvorsky, he also wrote for the piano. In 1922 he revealed himself as the true composer of the new works he had been introducing, and on 2 January 1924 the Philadelphia Orchestra devoted an entire concert to pieces by Josef Hofmann, alias Michel Dvorsky. From 1927 to 1938, when he resigned so that he could again devote his time to concertizing and composing, he was director of the Curtis Institute of Music in Philadelphia.

It was a festive occasion at the Metropolitan Opera House on 28 November 1937 when he gave a golden-jubilee concert celebrating his debut as a child prodigy fifty years before. Well-wishers in the audience included Fiorello La Guardia, Walter Damrosch, and the Ambassador of Poland. The President of the United States sent his congratulations. Perhaps the finest salute came from the reviewer in *The New York Times* who described the pianist's entrance onstage: "This was an artist, simple and modest and sincere, about to sit before his instrument and make music." Hofmann died in Los Angeles on 16 February 1957.

Josef Casimir Hofmann, 1876-1957

69. Josef Hofmann playing an encore, by Charles E. Chambers, undated.

Ruth Dennis began her dancing career about 1894 by auditioning in the foyer of Worth's Museum on Sixth Avenue in New York before a rather astonished ticket seller. She got a job and a two-week engagement of eleven performances a day. By 1899 she was off to London doing a bit part in *Zaza*, directed by David Belasco. It was while in one of Belasco's productions, and most certainly on a day when the flamboyant impresario was affecting clerical garb, that he elevated her to "St.-hood." A cigarette poster with an Egyptian theme suggested a whole new concept of dance theater to her, and slowly, but definitely, she began evolving a repertory of dances based on Oriental themes. Her success in New York and Boston was moderate compared to her achievement in Europe. After a slow start in Boston, she made headlines after her debut at the Marigny in Paris, 1 September 1906. Hers was an even greater triumph in Berlin; in Vienna the poet Hugo von Hofmannsthal called her dancing "incomparable." London was more enthusiastic the second time around, and, when she returned home in 1909, she came back a major American star. She had already won a place for herself as the third person of the dance trinity of the twentieth century—Loïe Fuller, Isadora Duncan, and Ruth St. Denis.

Ted Shawn was a young ministerial student when he first saw Ruth St. Denis dance in Denver in 1911. He was rather overcome by what he saw. He had begun dancing in his junior year in college, as physical therapy to counteract the effects of a paralysis from an attack of diphtheria. In 1914, within days after first approaching her to be her pupil, he was hired as her dance partner. They danced together onstage for the first time in Paducah, Kentucky, on 13 April 1914 and on 13 August they were married.

Their first joint choreography, *The Garden of Kama*, was danced in February of 1915. An estimate of their increasing popularity with American audiences can be documented in the fact that their portrait in costume was among the earliest color plates in the magazine that once ranked next only to the Holy Bible in most American homes—*The National Geographic*. In 1915 they founded in California the Denishawn School, an important nursery for the nurturing of the younger generation of American dancers. World War I interrupted the duo-career while Shawn served in the Army. Between 1922 and 1925 there was a series of most successful American tours. In the autumn of 1925 St. Denis and Shawn and company departed on a year-and-a-half tour of the Orient. They were applauded wherever they appeared and were accepted as eloquent evidence that America did indeed have culture as well as money.

Returning home in the spring of 1927, they found themselves of sufficient stature to badger the New York newspapers into creating posts for dance critics. Two such talents under one roof understandably led to discontent, and in 1931 they did not divorce, but went their separate ways except for some concert dates together.

Shawn, after teaching at Springfield College for a short while in 1932 and 1933, founded his internationally-lauded group, Ted Shawn and his Men Dancers. He had made the dance respectable as a profession for men. The troupe toured for seven years, giving over 1,200 performances in 750 cities. Shawn obtained property in western Massachusetts and from a lecture-demonstration session in July of 1933 developed the facilities into the site of one of the nation's foremost dance institutions. The annual summer Jacob's Pillow Dance Festival really began in 1942 with the opening of the Ted Shawn Theatre. Over a thousand dancers and dance companies have appeared there since, many

Ruth St. Denis, 1877-1968
Ted Shawn, 1891-1972

making their American debuts. More than 250 world premieres of choreographic works have occurred there.

"Miss Ruth," as she was affectionately called by those who loved her, made a comeback in 1937 after some years in shadow. In 1940 she opened her St. Denis School of Natya in New York, and in 1941 she danced at the Jacob's Pillow Dance Festival, a program duplicating a significant early success at New York's Hudson Theater thirty-five years before. At Jacob's Pillow in 1964 St. Denis and Shawn danced their last new duet together, "Siddhas of the Upper Air," in celebration of their golden wedding anniversary.

70. Ruth St. Denis, by Max Wieczorek, 1920.

71. Ted Shawn in his *Hopi Eagle Dance*, by
Albert Herter, 1925.

72. Ruth St. Denis in her *Peacock Dance*, by Robert Henri, 1919.

Six years after her birth in San Francisco on 28 May 1878, Isadora Duncan exhibited the first signs of her artistic precocity by teaching dancing to the children of her neighborhood. At age seventeen she traveled with her mother to Chicago and New York where impresarios had little enthusiasm for the young dancer's "new system" of interpretive dancing. Off to London by cattle boat, the entire Duncan family was discovered by the actress Mrs. Patrick Campbell and introduced to a more appreciative audience.

By the time Isadora returned to the United States in 1906, her creative new dance form had been applauded by private audiences in London and Paris, she had been for a while with Loïe Fuller's touring company, and she had made a triumphant solo tour of Munich, Berlin, Vienna, and Budapest. She had also attempted to build a temple of dance on a hill outside Athens and in 1904 opened a dancing school in the Berlin suburb of Grüunewald.

Isadora looked to antiquity as the inspiration for her dancing. When she returned for another American tour in late summer of 1908, the press accepted her dances as "classical," a reviewer in the *New York Sun* on 29 August calling her "the young woman who stepped down from a Grecian vase in the British Museum." No matter how fetching her movement onstage may have been, there were constant criticisms of her insistence on dancing to music not intended for the dance. Carl Van Vechten, in his *New York Times* review of a Duncan performance at the Metropolitan Opera House on 17 November 1909, protested against her "perverted use" of Beethoven's *Seventh Symphony* and in February of 1911 was still wondering why she insisted on dancing to music such as the "Liebestod" from Wagner's *Tristan und Isolde*. The artist John Sloan greatly admired her and saw

73. *Below:* A series of Abraham Walkowitz's sketches of Isadora Duncan dancing.

74. *Opposite page:* Isadora Duncan as photographed by Arnold Genthe about 1916.

Isadora Duncan, 1878-1927

this same performance on 15 February 1911. A portion of his diary entry for the day is both honest and enthusiastic:

> Isadora as she appears on that big simple stage seems like *all* womanhood—she looms big as the mother of the race. A heavy solid figure, large columnar legs, a solid high belly, breasts not too full and her head seems to be no more important than it should to give the body the chief place. In one of the dances she was absolutely nude save for a thin gauze drapery hanging from the shoulders. In none was she much clothed, simple filmy coverings usually with a loin cloth.

Hers was one of the most original and creative contributions to twentieth-century dance, and she generally found her audiences appreciative of her efforts. Tours of South America in 1916 and of this country again in 1917, however, were relatively unsuccessful, and she returned to Europe. In 1921 she accepted an invitation of the Soviet government to open a school in Moscow. She married the poet Sergei Yessenin there in 1922, and, when she returned to America with him, they were suspected of being Bolshevist propagandists. Her last trip here a failure, she bid farewell to an America she said knew nothing of "Love, Food, or Art," and she vowed never to return. In Paris in 1925 Yessenin committed suicide. The next two years were artistically barren for Isadora except for the writing and publication of her forthright biography, *My Life*. Its publication came just in time. At Nice, France, on 14 September 1927 she stepped into a sports car to go for a ride with a friend. The long scarf she was wearing caught in the back wheel of the car and she was garroted.

75. Isadora Duncan, etching by John Sloan, 1915. Sloan's color portrait of Isadora appears on p. 137.

She really wanted to be a concert pianist, but, born of a great theatrical family, Ethel Barrymore went on the stage instead. She made her stage debut in a bit part in *The Rivals,* and her apprenticeship included minor roles with her uncle, John Drew, in New York and with Sir Henry Irving's company in London. Although the critics in her hometown of Philadelphia were anything but kind when she opened there as Madame Trentoni in Clyde Fitch's *Captain Jinks of the Horse Marines,* Ethel Barrymore became a star when the play arrived at the Garrick Theatre in New York on 4 February 1901. Four weeks later her name was up in lights and stayed there throughout her long career. Her audiences adored her in light comedy and were disturbed when she attempted to break out of the stereotyped roles in which they revered her. They were perturbed in 1907 when she appeared as a scrubwoman in John Galsworthy's *The Silver Box,* although some of the professional critics were impressed, and in 1910 her acting of Zöe Blundell in Sir Arthur Pinero's *Midchannel* was only begrudgingly accepted as passable.

Her own tastes in the drama on the whole were rather conservative; she was not receptive to the more advanced playwrights. In 1905 she did appear in a production of Henrik Ibsen's *A Doll's House* with her brother John, but she found the Norwegian dramatist's characters perverted and false, and she dismissed George Bernard Shaw's plays as trivial. Her professional reputation was notably enhanced by her performance in Barrie's *Alice-Sit-by-the-Fire* in 1905, when she played a motherly role for the first time, and by her appearances in Somerset Maugham's *Lady Frederick* in 1908. Her critics and fans were especially happy when she returned to a lighter comedy part in Edna Ferber and G. V. Hobart's *Our Mrs. McChesney* in 1915. In 1919 she opened as Lady Helen Haden in Zöe Atkins' *Declassée,* a role particularly well suited to her talents.

Regally confident of her abilities, she saw nothing wrong with playing Juliet when she was forty-three and Ophelia and Portia when she was forty-six. Her playing of Lady Teazle in The Players' 1925 production of *School for Scandal* became one of the more brilliant facets of her career, and in the same year she was also well received for her acting in Somerset Maugham's *The Constant Wife.* By 1928 Ethel Barrymore was the undisputed "First Lady of the American Stage," and the Schuberts named a new theater in her honor, which she inaugurated on 20 December by opening as Sister Garcia in Martinez Sierra's *The Kindgom of God.*

Her motion picture debut, in the only film she ever made with both brothers John and Lionel, occured in 1933 in *Rasputin and the Empress.* In 1940 she almost refused the role of the Welsh schoolteacher Miss Moffat in Emlyn Williams' *The Corn is Green* as being unsuited for her. She played it, however, and it proved to be perhaps the finest performance of her career. As her health failed she spent more and more time in California.

In 1950 she returned to Broadway to act in a benefit performance for the American National Theater and Academy. At the fall of the curtain, a grand ovation forced her to take several curtain calls. Acknowledging the applause, she said, "You make it sound inviting." These were her last words on the Broadway stage. She returned to Hollywood, where she died 18 June 1959.

Ethel Barrymore, 1879-1959

76. *Above*: John, Ethel, and Lionel Barrymore, 1904.

77. *Opposite page*: Ethel Barrymore as Madame Trentoni in Clyde Fitch's *Captain Jinks of the Horse Marines*, by Sigismund de Ivanowski, probably painted in 1901.

Born in Yalta, Russia, on 4 June 1879, Alla Nazimova was a music student for a short time before she entered the Academy of Acting in Moscow. In 1904 she joined the theatrical company of Paul Orleneff and toured with it, making her New York debut on 23 March 1905 in a Russian language production of Chirikov's *The Chosen People*. The American portion of its tour a failure, the company returned to Russia, but Nazimova remained behind.

On 13 November 1906 she made her English language debut at New York's Princess Theatre in Ibsen's *Hedda Gabler*. She followed close on the heels of Mrs. Fiske as a champion of the Norwegian dramatist. In 1907 she appeared in *A Doll's House* and in *The Master Builder* with Walter Hampden. In 1910 she was first seen in *Little Eyolf*. It was her appearances in what one critic called her "lust-and-vengeance-dramas" such as *Comet*, *The Passion Flower*, and *Bella Donna* that first really claimed the attention of the American public. Between 1916 and 1923 she appeared in a number of motion pictures, including *A Doll's House*, *Camille*, and a famed production of Oscar Wilde's *Salome* designed à la Beardsley by Natacha Rambova. In 1918 Nazimova received special acclaim for a series of three Ibsen plays, which added *The Wild Duck* to revivals of *Hedda Gabler* and the inevitable *A Doll's House*.

An undisputed high point of her career was her creation of the role of Christine in the Theatre Guild's production of Eugene O'Neill's *Mourning Becomes Electra*, which premiered in New York on 26 October 1931. Robert Benchley in his review of the first performance wrote, "Nazimova, in spite of her Russian accent . . . made so much of the sinning Clytemnestra (Christine) that the drama lost much when she withdrew into the shade of the House of Mannon never to return."

Her acting of Mrs. Alving in her touring production of Ibsen's *Ghosts* in the 1935-1936 season prompted some critics to compare her with Duse. The title role in *Hedda Gabler* was now considered her property, and she opened her fourth and last run in the drama at the Longacre Theatre on 16 November 1936. When it closed she had, as the ill-fated Hedda, committed suicide on Broadway 128 times. She was last seen on the New York stage in April of 1939 in Karel Capek's *The Mother*. Her artistic endeavors shifted again to the cinema. She died in Hollywood 13 July 1945.

Alla Nazimova, 1879-1945

78. *Left*: Alla Nazimova in *Hedda Gabler*, probably 1936.
79. *Below*: Nazimova in a theatrical pose, by Edward Simmons, 1915.

Born in Brooklyn on 30 June 1879, Walter Hampden Dougherty made one of his first appearances onstage there as Shylock in a Brooklyn Polytechnic Institute production when he was sixteen years old. He dropped his family name for stage purposes and went to England for his theatrical apprenticeship, making his debut at Brighton on 2 September 1901. Three years later he was acting with the repertory company at London's Adelphi Theatre and in May of 1905 replaced Sir Henry Irving for one week in the role of Hamlet. Returning to New York, he was engaged by Henry Miller to support Alla Nazimova and first appeared with her on 2 September 1907 as Count Silvio in *The Comtesse Couquette*. In the same season he appeared with her in *The Master Builder* and in *A Doll's House*. In March of 1908 Hampden created the role of Manson in Charles Rann Kennedy's *The Servant in the House*. In 1916, the tercentenary of Shakespeare's death, he played Caliban in a notable revival of *The Tempest*. He was at his peak two years later when in March and April of 1918 he played Elihu in *The Book of Job*, Jokanaan in Oscar Wilde's *Salome*, and Marc Anthony and Oberon in more familiar works by Shakespeare.

On 22 November 1918 he opened at the Plymouth Theatre in *Hamlet*. Critic Clayton Hamilton, claiming he had seen all the Hamlets on the English-speaking stage since Edwin Booth, called Hampden the greatest living interpreter of the "Melancholy Dane." Shylock, the role essayed in his Brooklyn debut, was added to his professional repertory while on tour in 1920. Rostand's long-nosed, but romantic hero Cyrano de Bergerac became another of his greatest characterizations when he opened at New York's National Theatre in a new version by Brian Hooker on 1 November 1923. It played 250 performances in that house before he took it on tour.

In 1925 he leased the Colonial Theatre, and renaming it Hampden's Theatre, opened in *Hamlet* with Ethel Barrymore as his Ophelia. Two years later he became the fourth president of The Players, succeeding Edwin Booth, Joseph Jefferson, and John Drew. Although by tradition the presidency was an office held for life, Walter Hampden relinquished the title on 8 October 1954. He made his first appearance on television as Macbeth in the Hallmark Playhouse production and appeared for the last time on Broadway as Deputy-Governor Danforth in Arthur Miller's *The Crucible* in October 1953. In Hollywood to make a motion picture, he was stricken while on his way to the Metro-Goldwyn-Mayer studios and died in Cedars of Lebanon Hospital on 11 June 1955.

Walter Hampden, 1879-1955

80, 81. Walter Hampden in the title role of Shakespeare's *Hamlet*, by William Glackens, 1917, and the artist's pastel sketch for the portrait.

The inheritor of generations of theatrical tradition, John Barrymore did not originally want to be an actor. He really wanted to be a painter, and it was only after unsuccessful attempts as a painter and illustrator that he, like his older sister Ethel, turned to the stage. The tales of his erratic behavior onstage and offstage in the years of his apprenticeship reflect the lack of seriousness in his calling in the early days. His first appearance onstage was as a substitute for an indisposed actor during the Philadelphia tryout of his sister's first great hit, *Captain Jinks of the Horse Marines*. He muffed his lines, but, unabashed, he took a solo curtain call. As befitted his attitude, most of his early roles were in a lighter vein. His first substantial role was as Max in a production of Hermann Sudermann's *Magda* in Chicago in October of 1903. Two months later he played New York for the first time when he opened at the Savoy Theatre as Corley in *Glad of It*. He matured a bit as an actor when he appeared as Charley Hine in Richard Harding Davis's *The Dictator* at New York's Criterion Theatre on 4 April 1904. He played his first major role in Rida Johnson Young's *The Boys of Company B* in the spring of 1907, and the only musical role of his career in *A Stubborn Cinderella* early in 1909. On 4 September 1909 he opened in New York as Nat Duncan in Winchell Smith's *The Fortune Hunter* and found himself a star.

In 1916 he made his first venture into serious dramatic acting when he appeared in John Galsworthy's *Justice*, both in New York and on tour. His birth as a romantic star came with his first appearance in the title role of John Raphael's *Peter Ibbetson*, which premiered at the Republic Theatre on 17 April 1917. With him in the cast was his older brother Lionel. In 1819 he acted in a revival of Leo Tolstoi's *Redemption* which ran on Broadway for 204 performances. The following year he appeared again opposite his brother in *The Jest* by Sam Benelli.

With painstaking thoroughness John Barrymore prepared for his first Shakespearean role, Richard III, in 1920. He put himself in the hands of an able coach to prepare his voice and his delivery of the lengthy verse passages. The costuming of his Richard was meticulous. He had two suits of full-weight armor made to order and he conferred with experts at the British Museum regarding the design of the armor and a sword he was to carry onstage. He considered the role of the deformed king the first "genuine acting" he had done. Dramatically, it was one of the two pinnacles of his career. The second, even loftier, was his reading of the melancholy Prince of Denmark. John Barrymore's *Hamlet* opened at the Sam H. Harris Theatre on 16 November 1922. In his review in the *Herald* the following day, Alexander Woollcott gave the venture his pontifical blessing when he wrote, "One who has seen all the *Hamlets* that have been given in this country in the last twenty-five years must give over the very front of his report to the conviction that this new one is the finest of them all."

In 1925 John Barrymore left the stage to devote all his time to work in motion pictures where his famed profile became one of the shining ornaments of the silver screen. He returned to the stage only once, in 1939 in *My Dear Children*, to play a character who was a pathetic caricature of himself in his declining years. He died in Hollywood on 29 May 1942.

John Barrymore's career was catalogued by the camera from early in his career. There is also a handsome and colorful painting of him reciting the "Alas, poor Yorick!" speech by James Montgomery Flagg, the noted illustrator. It appropriately shows the famous Barrymore profile. Barrymore himself was an able caricaturist and left a wealth of self-portrait drawings in various roles.

John Barrymore, 1882-1942

82. John Barrymore in the title role of Shakespeare's *Hamlet*, by
James Montgomery Flagg, about 1923.

83. John Barrymore and Blanche Yerka in *Hamlet*, 1922. One of
Barrymore's self-portrait caricatures appears on p. 141.

XII. Dorothy Stickney as Vinnie in Howard Lindsay and Russell Crouse's *Life with Father* by John Falter, 1940. A true "theater picture," the portrait shows the actress behind the set about to make her entrance. To paint it, the artist duplicated the stage lighting in his studio.

XIII. Fay Bainter as the Willow Princess in Benrimo and Harrison
Rhodes's *The Willow Tree* by Robert Henri, 1918.

XIV. Tallulah Bankhead as Wanda Myro in Arthur Wimperis's play
He's Mine, by Augustus John, 1930.

84. Self-portrait caricature of John Barrymore, 1920. It is thought
that the actor has shown himself as Peter Ibbetson, with Ibbetson's
alter ego in the background.

Anna Pavlova was ten years old when she was accepted into the Imperial School of Ballet in her native St. Petersburg, Russia, in 1891. She made her first stage appearance at a benefit for one of her teachers while still a student, and in 1899, upon completion of her training, was taken into the Imperial Ballet as a coryphée. By 1906 she was a prima ballerina.

The following year she received a leave of absence to appear outside of Russia for the first time. She toured Europe for portions of three seasons and in 1909 appeared with Diaghilev's Ballets Russes during its Paris season. Her association with this revolutionary force in the history of ballet, however, was so short-lived as to have no effect upon her attitudes toward the dance, which were essentially those of a virtuoso dancer rather than of a dance pioneer.

In January of 1910 she appeared for the first time in America during a month-long season of ballet at the Metropolitan Opera House. She and her premier danseur, Mikhail Mordkin, were an immediate success, for it had been decades since the New York public had seen dancers of their caliber. She returned to the United States again in the season of 1910-1911 for an extensive tour and was already being written about as one who was to become a legendary figure in dance history. Reviewing her dancing of *The Dying Swan*, an incidental number danced to music from Camille Saint-Saëns' *Carnival of the Animals*, and a dance which was virtually her trademark, a critic of the *Boston Evening Times* wrote: "Here was the dance of the phantom of a dream, stirring into misty and lingering vision, while out of flesh and blood, with imagination for the music and technical skill for the wand, Miss Pavlova wrought its gossamer beauty." Heady reporting, indeed.

Anna Pavlova's personality and artisty entranced her audiences wherever she appeared, and she became a primary force in the popularization of ballet in the United States. Her role in the evolution of the modern dance was negligible, but her extended tours brought the dance in its classic beauty to millions who otherwise might never have discovered it. In 1913 she resigned from the company in St. Petersburg's Maryinsky Theatre and left Russia never to return.

During the years of World War I she toured only in North and South America. From 1914 until 1930 she traveled with her company to almost every part of the civilized world. It is estimated that the sum total of her professional travels was well over 5,000,000 miles. It can be rightly said that Pavlova, among all the dancers of our century, did the most to open our world to ballet. During the midst of a European epidemic of influenza, Anna Pavlova died at The Hague on 23 January 1931. She was cremated and her ashes were interred in London where she had resided since 1912. An American newspaper reporting her death looked back nostalgically and called her "the fine flower of an age that was already passing when this lovely blossom appeared."

Anna Pavlova, 1881-1931

85. Malvina Hoffman's 1912 bronze group of Anna Pavlova and
Mikhail Mordkin, entitled *Bacchanale Russe*, one of several she did of
the two dancers, both clothed and nude.

Born in Melrose, Massachusetts, 28 February 1882, Geraldine Farrar went to Europe to taste her first stage success. She made her debut with the Berlin Opera on 15 October 1901. Her voice and beauty made her an immediate favorite. Much to the chagrin of the director of the Opera, Miss Farrar's special patronage by the royal family granted her a dispensation to sing her roles in Italian while the rest of the company sang in the usual German.

Her debut at the Metropolitan Opera House on 26 November 1906, at age twenty-four, as the heroine in the Charles Gounod setting of Shakespeare's *Romeo and Juliet*, was highly anticipated by critics and public alike. Henry Krehbiel's review in the *New York Tribune* anticipated the public attitude which was to persist throughout Farrar's Met career: ". . . she achieved a place among those whom a Metropolitan audience recognized as in the forefront of the world's operatic artists."

For almost twenty years Geraldine Farrar and Enrico Caruso reigned jointly as the most profitable and popular singers on the Metropolitan roster. Her voice was admired, but critics went into raptures over her acting as the Goose Girl in Engelbert Humperdinck's *Königskinder* (she insisted on performing with live geese) and of the title roles in Leoncavallo's *Zaza* and in Bizet's *Carmen*. At her first performance as Zaza on 16 January 1920, her loyal following of young female fans, called "gerryflappers" by the press, went into hysterics, and J. G. Huneker, critic for the *New York World*, claimed that "Zaza in the role of Geraldine Farrar is a sensation. . . . She had taken possession of the physical habitation of Geraldine Farrar; therefore she was beautiful, therefore she was reborn with a golden throat. . . . There is only one role. She is Zaza. Zaza is Farrar."

She was the first operatic luminary to acknowledge the existence of motion pictures and capped her short career in that medium with a characterization of the savior of France in an epic entitled *Joan the Woman*. On 22 April 1922 she sang her last performance at the Metropolitan, an emotionally received Zaza, and then retired from the operatic stage at age forty, as she always said she would. She died in Ridgefield, Connecticut, 11 March 1967.

Geraldine Farrar, 1882-1967

86. *Opposite page:* Geraldine Farrar, by Friedrich August von Kaulbach, 1904. This portrait appears in color on p. 69.

87, 88. *Left:* Farrar as the Goose Girl in a German production of Engelbert Humperdinck's *Königskinder*. *Above:* Publicity still of the singer in the motion picture version of *Carmen*, 1915.

John McCormack's public singing career began during his student days at Sligo College, and in 1904 the young tenor won a gold medal at the National Irish Festival in Dublin. Shortly afterward, he appeared in America for the first time on a short concert tour. Returning to Europe, he went to Italy for serious study and made his debut in opera in Savona in Pietro Mascagni's *L'Amico Fritz* in December of 1905.

Neither Ireland nor England took notice of him until he appeared on 1 March 1907 at one of the Queen's Hall ballad concerts arranged by the London publisher Arthur Boosey. The result of this and subsequent concerts was his debut at Covent Garden on 15 October 1907 as Turridu in Mascagni's *Cavalleria rusticana.* Later in the same season he appeared in Verdi's *Rigoletto* and Mozart's *Don Giovanni.* On 10 November 1909 McCormack made his American operatic debut at Oscar Hammerstein's Manhattan Opera House singing Alfredo in Verdi's *La Traviata.* From that time on McCormack was a conspicuous and beloved part of the American musical scene. He became a member of the Boston Opera Company in 1910, and from 1912 to 1914 he sang in opera in Boston and Philadelphia. He also made several appearances at the Metropolitan Opera and began his long and almost legendary career on the American concert stage.

Rather light-voiced for opera, McCormack really excelled as a recitalist. In 1917 Olin Downes wrote of his concert singing: "his mastery included the clear enunciation of the English language, and the making of this tongue beautiful in song." During World War I he devoted much of his time to recitals to raise money for wartime charities and for Liberty Bond sales, and in 1919 he became a citizen of the United States, the country that had done so much to further his career. In concert he always sang to a sold-out house; his sale of phonograph records was second only to Caruso's. McCormack himself considered his recording of "Il mio tesoro" from *Don Giovanni* his finest effort for the phonograph.

A new song was assured of success if it appeared on a McCormack program. His recital repertory was light on operatic selections and consisted primarily of the classic airs of oratorio, of *lieder*, and of Irish songs, sung in so masterful a manner as to elevate them above the realm of the simple and popular. Like his friend Fritz Kreisler, he was accused by some critics of cheapening his art with light music. John McCormack, however, appreciated the adulation of his public and went on giving them what they wanted and enjoyed. Except for a slight period of inactivity in 1922, because of illness, his concert tours continued until his retirement in 1937. He returned to his native country, Ireland, and lived there until his death on 16 September 1945.

John McCormack, 1884-1945

89. John McCormack, by Sir William Orpen, painted in 1923.

On November 8, 1939 Howard Lindsay and Russel Crouse's *Life with Father* opened at New York's Empire Theatre for a record-breaking run of 3,224 performances. All the critics loved it except the person writing for *The Daily Worker*. With dedication of purpose, that writer declared *Life with Father* a "Vindication of Life of Leisure," and judged that "the Play May Be Good Propaganda, But It's Certainly Bad Art." The less prejudiced made kinder pronouncements. Brooks Atkinson in *The New York Times* called it "A perfect comedy" and an "authentic part of our American folklore." In the *New York Daily Mirror* Walter Winchell complimented three noted comediennes when he wrote that "Dorothy Stickney essays the role of Mrs. Day as Bille Burke and Gracie Allen would toy with it. This combination, you can easily imagine, makes for hilarious amusement."

In the summer of 1921, just after graduation from the Northwestern Dramatic School im Minneapolis, Dorothy Stickney made her stage debut with a quartet called the "Southern Belles." Her New York stage debut came when she opened in *The Squall*. The play was short-lived, and on 30 December 1926 she opened at the Music Box as Liz in Maurine Watkins' *Chicago*, a melodrama about a travesty of justice. After a reprise which included some gentle acting in a revival of *The Beaux Stratagem*, another juicy role as a big-city hussy came her way when she opened in the late summer of 1928 as Mollie Molloy in Charles MacArthur and Ben Hecht's *The Front Page*. Eleven years after that characterization and twelve after marrying Howard Lindsay, Dorothy Stickney created the role of Vinnie in *Life with Father*. It will always be remembered as her greatest contribution to the American stage.

So sympathetic was her playing of Vinnie that a sequel, *Life with Mother*, was written by the same authors. It opened at the Empire on October 20, 1948, again starring Howard Lindsay and Dorothy Stickney in their original characters of Mr. and Mrs. Day. Brooks Atkinson found the sequel in some respects "more beguiling" than the original. But during the Second World War, American tastes had changed, and *Life with Mother* had a relatively short run of only 265 performances.

Together, Lindsay and Crouse had already collaborated on *State of the Union* in 1934 and were later to work together on *Arsenic and Old Lace*, which ran on Broadway from 1941 to 1944, and *Call Me Madam* (1950), *The Sound of Music* (1959) and *The President* (1962).

Lindsay had entered Harvard University to become a Unitarian minister. He left it to enter a life in the theater. Afte six months at the American Academy of Dramatic Arts, he made his professional debut in a road show in 1909. Soon he was on the West Coast in vaudeville, burlesque, and silent films. After tours of duty with the Margaret Anglin company of actors and the 76th Division in World War I, he was back in New York. His career there really began in 1921 when he both directed and acted in *Dulcy*, a hit starring Lynn Fontanne.

Howard Lindsay's service to the American theater was recognized by his peers when he was elected the fifth president of The Players. He presided from 1955 until he resigned in 1965. His importance was recognized by thousands of others who most likely never saw him on stage when his front-page obituary appeared in *The New York Times* on February 12, 1968: "No one who saw Howard Lindsay as Clarence Day, the irascible but lovable Father in 'Life With Father,' ever thought of him as anything else."

Aside from the albums of photos that were made of the play during its record run on Broadway, there are two handsome painted souvenirs of the production and its two stars. One is the Paul

Howard Lindsay, 1889-1968
Dorothy Stickney, 1900 -

Meltsner painting of Father and Mother and of one of the pugs that figured so conspicuously in the play, and the other is John Falter's handsome canvas of Miss Stickney alone about to make her entrance. Both paintings were painted as a result of the artists' interest in the prototypically American play.

90. Howard Lindsay and Dorothy Stickney as Father and Mother Day in *Life with Father*, by Paul Meltsner, c. 1940. John Falter's portrait of Dorothy Stickney appears in color on p. 138.

Born in Copenhagen on 20 March 1890, Lauritz Melchior made his operatic debut as a baritone at the Royal Opera House in his native city on 2 April 1912. Convinced by his colleagues that he was really a tenor, he pursued further studies and made his second debut, again at the Royal Opera, on 8 October 1918 in Wagner's *Tannhäuser*. Concentrating on Wagnerian roles, he appeared for the first time as Siegmund in London's Covent Garden in May of 1924 and two months later in the title role in *Parsifal* at Bayreuth.

It was as Tannhäuser that he sang for the first time at the Metropolitan Opera House during a matinee performance on 17 February 1926. His debut was overshadowed by the excitement attending the debut that night of the American soprano Marion Talley, and he was coolly received. One critic found his voice "forced and rough." Melchior became gradually more comfortable on the stage of the Met, however, and it became slowly obvious to all who heard him that he was the "Heldentenor" the New York company had been seeking for years. Wagner again received his due in New York, and it was Melchior's prerogative to be leading man to the principal Wagnerian sopranos of his time. On 16 January 1933 he was Tristan to Frida Leider's Isolde at the latter's Metropolitan debut. He assisted Lotte Lehmann at her debut on 11 January 1934 in *Die Walküre*—he was Siegmund to her Sieglinde—and on 28 December 1939 he played the same unknowingly incestuous sibling at Helen Traubel's debut. The Norwegian soprano Kirsten Flagstad debuted at the Metropolitan on 2 February 1935, and, three days later, Lauritz Melchior sang *Tristan and Isolde* with her for the first time. With these two stalwart singers in the roles of the unhappy lovers, the Wagner masterpiece assumed unprecedented popularity at the old Broadway house of the venerable Met. In a review, dated 23 December 1936, W. J. Henderson called Melchior's Tristan "the best the Metropolitan had known since Jean de Reszke." There could hardly be higher praise.

Melchior's 200th performance of the role occurred on the Met stage on 4 December 1944, and in 1946 he celebrated twenty years with the company by singing a gala Sunday concert on the anniversary date of his debut. The proceeds he donated to a fund for a new production of Wagner's *Ring* cycle. His last appearance at the Metropolitan was as Lohengrin on 2 February 1950. Although he had retired from the operatic stage, his career had not ended. He appeared frequently in concert, on television, and, following the example of one of his leading ladies, in nightclubs. His singing roles in motion pictures brought opera to many who otherwise might never have discovered it.

He died in Santa Monica, California, on March 18, 1973.

91. *Opposite page:* Lauritz Melchior as Tristan in Richard Wagner's *Tristan und Isolde*, by Nikol Schattenstein, 1937. The artist has shown the fateful moment in act 1 when Tristan is about to drink the love potion offered by Isolde.

Lauritz Melchior, 1890-1973

Born in the Midwest on 26 June 1890, Jeanne Eagels came into show business by way of a touring Dubinsky Brothers' tent show when she was fifteen. By the time she made it to New York, impresario David Belasco described her eyes as "hard and bitter, but shining with ambition." She first attracted the attention of Broadway theatergoers when she appeared as Miss Renault in the 1911 production of a play entitled *Jumping Jupiter*. Most of the plays in which she appeared are now mentioned only in the most scholarly anthologies of Broadway productions. One was notable, however —a revival of *Disraeli* in which she played under George Arliss in his most famous role—and she had a 340-performance run beginning 5 September 1918 when she opened in *Daddies* at the Belasco Theatre.

These plays are all overshadowed, however, by her one spectacular triumph. At Maxine Elliott's Theatre on 7 November 1922 she created the role of Sadie Thompson in John Colton's and Clemence Randolph's adaptation of Somerset Maugham's story, *Miss Thompson*. The play, with Jeanne Eagels as the wayward prostitute Sadie, was the dramatic triumph of the 1922-1923 New York season. John Dorbin's *New York Times* review of the opening-night performance on 7 November 1922 described Miss Engels's acting as having "an emotional power as fiery and unbridled in effect as it is artistically restrained" and noted that "The house . . . fairly rose to Miss Eagels and acclaimed her." *Rain* played for 648 performances.

The remainder of her career was downhill. On 21 March 1927 she opened in *Her Cardboard Lover* at the Empire Theatre for a run that lasted 152 performances. The next season the play went on tour. She failed to appear at a performance in Milwaukee and then again in St. Louis; four days later she left the show, forcing the producers to cancel the remainder of the tour. Early in April of 1928 Actors' Equity Association barred her from the stage. She ruined both her health and career through overindulgence in alcohol and drugs, and on 3 October 1929 she collapsed and died at the Park Avenue Hospital during a routine physical examination.

Jeanne Eagels, 1890-1929

92. Jeanne Eagels as Sadie
Thompson in *Rain*, by Guy
Pene du Bois, 1922.

Although Lynn Fontanne made her professional debut in a Christmas pantomime at London's Drury Lane Theatre on 26 December 1905 and Alfred Lunt made his at the Castle Square Theatre in Boston on 7 October 1912, the summer of 1919 is a more monumental calendar landmark for them. It was at this time, in Washington, D.C., that they first acted together. There are few times when one of them was a success in a production that did not also star the other. Alfred Lunt's portrayal of the title role in *Clarence* in 1919 and Miss Fontanne's achievements as Eliza Doolittle in the Theatre Guild production of Shaw's *Pygmalion* in 1926 are exceptions to the rule.

Lunt and Fontanne are the most famous dramatic duo in the history of the American stage. Their drawing power made secure even erstwhile flops. A failure when it was first produced in New York, *The Guardsman* was revived by the Theatre Guild in October of 1924 and, with the Lunts as stars, became the first of that organization's productions to make money. From then on many of the Lunts' triumphs were to be in Guild productions, such as *The Goat Song* (1926), *Elizabeth the Queen* (1930), *Idiot's Delight* (1936), and *Amphitryon 38* (1937). In that same year, 1937, Alfred Lunt directed and they both starred in a Guild production of Shakespeare's *Taming of the Shrew*. It was a hit both in New York and on tour. Their appearance in Terence Rattigan's *O Mistress Mine* saved the Theatre Guild's 1945-1946 season from financial disaster. They had played it first in London under the title *Love in Idleness* and, after opening under the new title in New York on 23 January 1946, took it on to even further success on tour.

Their performance as a team of mind readers in *The Great Sebastians* was seen by millions when it went from stage to television production in 1957. On 5 May 1958 the Globe Theatre was reopened in New York as the Lunt-Fontanne Theatre with the titular saints of the building shining forth in the opening night production of Friedrich Dürrenmatt's *The Visit*. On 4 July 1964 they received jointly, as is only fitting and proper, the President's Medal of Freedom.

Alfred Lunt, 1892-1977
Lynn Fontanne, ?-

93. Lynn Fontanne and Alfred Lunt, by James Fosburgh, 1957.

Mae West was born in Brooklyn and went on the stage for the first time in 1897. In the next twenty-nine years she appeared in a succession of productions, most memorable only because she can be listed as one of the cast.

Then came 1926 and *Sex*. The play opened at Daly's Theatre in New York on April 26. Despite the fact that no newspaper would run an ad for it because of its title, it ran for 375 performances. It was also declared unfit for human attention—for reasons apparently more political than moral—and so Miss West, her manager, and her producer were arrested. Although she claims to have found the courtroom as theater slightly less amusing than the stage, the judge sentenced all three to fines and to ten days in jail. The publicity generated by her imprisonment on Welfare Island did her career no harm.

The following year her own play, *The Drag*, opened in Paterson, New Jersey; and Brooklyn, during Holy Week of 1928, saw the first performance of her *Diamond Lil*. The play moved on to New York's Royale Theatre and got quite a bit of attention from red-cheeked critics. *The New York Times's* reviewer found Miss West's story of Bowery lowlife " . . . simply, if somewhat embarassingly entertaining for two of its three acts. The third one is pretty bad." As he also admitted, "She is a good actress, is Miss West . . . ."

Mae West, 1892-

In 1932, at the age of forty, Mae West went to Hollywood and by 1935 was its highest paid screen actress. In 1943, with her hour-glass figure somewhat eclipsed by Betty Grable's legs and Lana Turner's sweaters, she rested awhile, and then, in her sixties, she appeared once more in night club acts and on tour with some of her earlier plays. With her usual penchant for the showiest of showmanship, her diminutive form was frequently framed by musclemen.

In 1970 she was persuaded to appear in a movie version of Gore Vidal's novel *Myra Breckenridge*. She wrote her own scenes and stole the show. She came to the New York premiere attired as a reigning queen. It is said that a crowd of 10,000 roared a rousing welcome as she was helped from her limousine.

Her protrait by Dali seems to have been an impromptu act of devotion or whim on the part of the artist. It is thought to have been painted about 1934 and may be a photo or a magazine page overworked in gouache. The one artist has turned the other into an opulent drawing room with a tour de force of illusionism that salutes a tour de force of center stage.

94. Mae West and company on stage in *Diamond Lil*, 1955. Salvador Dali's portrait of the inimitable Miss West appears on p. 176.

Born in Los Angeles on 7 December 1892, Fay Bainter made her stage debut at age six in a stock company production of a play called *The Jewess*. After further appearances in stock, musical repertory, and vaudeville, she made her New York debut as Celine in *The Rose of Panama* at Daly's Theatre on 22 January 1912.

Her first hit was in *The Willow Tree* as the Japanese princess, an idol that came to life. The play was not a particularly good one, but the critics liked Miss Bainter. The day after the opening on 6 March 1917 at the Cohan and Harris Theatre, the *New York Times* review carried the headline "Fay Bainter Acts with Rare Tenderness and Witchery a Play Now Overlong and Overtricky." Artist Robert Henri preserved her appearance in this role in a charming painting and admired her as well in the next production in which she starred. Of her first appearance in *The Kiss Burglar*, 9 May 1918, he wrote to a friend in Toledo: "Last night Fay Bainter was a delight to us and all the rest of the audience . . . . She put beauty into musical comedy, and I hope she has put it there to stay."

She achieved stardom in another Oriental role in *East is West*, which opened in New York on Christmas Day, 1918, and later toured until 1922. In 1927 she made another cross-country tour in a vaudeville presentation entitled *Great Moments in Great Plays*. Special acclaim came her way for her performances in *Lysistrata*, *For Services Rendered*, and *Dodsworth* in the early thirties. She never aspired to Shakespeare, but some of her characterizations were cast from the classic mold of tragedy. She played Amanda in Tennessee Williams's *The Glass Menagerie* for the first time in 1955 at Houston's Alley Theatre, and she was Mary Cavan Tyrone in the touring company of O'Neill's *Long Day's Journey into Night* in the season of 1957-1958. Among her numerous motion-picture roles, the most notable was that of Auntie Belle in *Jezebel*, a performance which won her an Academy Award in 1938. She died 16 April 1968.

95. *Opposite page*: Fay Bainter as the Willow Princess in *The Willow Tree*, by Robert Henri, 1918. This portrait appears in color on p. 139.

Fay Bainter, 1892-1968

When he was three years old, Clifton Webb and his family moved to New York from Indianapolis, where he was born on 19 November 1893. By way of a dancing class, he made his stage debut in 1900 as Cholly in a Carnegie Hall children's theatrical entitled *The Brownies*. In the next production of the same small company he had a title role, that of Oliver Twist in a dramatization of the Dickens novel. Leaving school, he studied painting with Robert Henri and voice with the baritone Victor Maurel. In this teens he made his operatic debut in Boston as Laertes in a production of Ambroise Thomas's *Mignon*.

On 7 April 1913 Clifton Webb appeared in his first light opera in New York when he opened in *The Purple Road* at Maxine Elliott's Theatre for a run of 136 performances. For a while he was a partner to Bonnie Glass and later to Mae Murray and became second in popularity as a ballroom dancer only to the famed duo of Irene and Vernon Castle. His first appearance on Broadway in a musical was in Cole Porter and T. Lawrason Rigg's *See America First*, a spoof of George M. Cohan's flag-waving shows. It did not find favor with a flag-waving public and lasted only fifteen performances. A series of shows between 1917 and 1921, *Love O'Mike*, *Listen Lester*, and *As You Were*, found him fully established in his audiences' favor as a dancer.

Two successful seasons in London and Paris followed, and then Clifton Webb returned to New York in John Murray Anderson's *Jack and Jill*, which opened a ninety-two-performance run at the Globe Theatre on 22 March 1923. Later the same year he played his first straight comedy role in *Meet the Wife* at the Klaw Theatre. George S. Kaufman in reviewing it stated that "Mr. Webb will never have to put on his dancing shoes again." He did, however, when he appeared in the musical *Sunny* at the New Amsterdam Theatre in the fall and winter of 1925 and in a number of shows in which he starred during the next eight years. Notable among them were Rodgers and Hart's *She's My Baby* and George Gershwin's *Treasure Girl* in 1928, *Three's a Crowd* in 1930, and *Flying Colors* in 1932. Opening at the Music Box Theatre on 30 September 1933 in Moss Hart and Irving Berlin's *As Thousands Cheer*, Webb gave a bravura performance alongside cohorts Ethel Waters and Marilyn Miller and then returned to the West Coast for his first stay in Hollywood. In the entire eighteen months he was there—under a contract paying a reputed 3,000 a week—he never made one movie.

Back he went to Broadway for a nondancing role, opening on 12 October 1936 at the Guild Theatre in *And Stars Remain*. In 1939 he starred in an important revival of Oscar Wilde's *The Importance of Being Earnest*; he followed its run with a year and a half on tour as Sheridan Whiteside in Moss Hart and George S. Kaufman's satire on critic Alexander Woollcott, *The Man Who Came to Dinner*. On the eve of World War II he opened at the Morosco Theatre as the harassed hero of Noël Coward's *Blithe Spirit*, a play which gave a sadly needed touch of lightness to a trying time and ran for 650 performances. Most of his talent from that time on was exhibited for the benefit of Hollywood motion-picture cameras.

A notable return to Broadway was marked by the actor's presence in Coward's *Present Laughter*, which opened at the Plymouth Theatre on 29 October 1946. Clifton Webb died on 13 October 1966 in Beverly Hills.

96. *Opposite page*: Clifton Webb, by Walter Dean Goldbeck, before 1925.

Clifton Webb, 1893-1966

The daughter of a medical student from Buffalo, Katharine Cornell was born in Berlin, Germany, on 16 February 1898. Her New York stage debut was made as a Japanese mother in the Washington Square Players' production of *Bushido* at the Comedy Theatre on 13 November 1916. Her entire part consisted of only four words. Other minor roles followed before she joined a stock company which played Buffalo and Detroit. After a half dozen ingenue parts, she played her first lead role in a 1915 production of *The Man Who Came Back*, and on 20 November 1919 she made her London debut in a dramatization of Louisa May Alcott's *Little Women*. Returning home, she played Diane in *Seventh Heaven* in Detroit and returned to New York in 1921.

She had her first real personal triumph when she played Sydney Fairfield in Clemence Dane's *Bill of Divorcement* that same year, and her name went up in lights when she opened as Iris March in Michael Arlen's *The Green Hat* at the Broadhurst Theatre on 15 September 1925. On 12 December 1924 she opened at the 48th Street Theatre in the title role of George Bernard Shaw's *Candida*. Reviewing the opening-night performance in *The New York Times*, Stark Young wrote that "Candida in the hands of Katharine Cornell was a deep revelation of the part. Her frail presence had something in it of the light of another world." Heywood Broun in the *World* observed that "The Candida of Katharine Cornell is the finest performance she has yet given for our theatre. It is bright with a steady flame. It is beautiful to look at and beautiful to feel." Each season after that she returned to Broadway and added to her laurels.

From 1931 she appeared only under her own management. On 9 February 1931 she opened at the Empire Theatre as Elizabeth Barrett in Rudolf Besier's *The Barretts of Wimpole Street*, which ran 372 performances and toured until July of 1932. This role became a staple in her repertory, and she played it again on tour in the season of 1933-1934, alternating it with *Candida* and *Romeo and Juliet*, which Brooks Atkinson called a "stunning production." In February of 1935 she opened again in New York as Elizabeth Barrett. She added another Shaw play to her credits when she played his *St. Joan* for the first time in March of 1936. In 1937 and 1942 she again revived *Candida* and during the war years toured with *The Barretts of Wimpole Street* in performances for military audiences in Europe. On 26 November 1947 she added another sterling characterization of a Shakespearean heroine to her checklist of successes when she opened at the Martin Beck Theatre in *Antony and Cleopatra* for the longest run the play had ever had, 126 performances. In the season of 1951-1952 she appeared in a notable revival of *The Constant Wife* by Somerset Maugham, and, in 1959 and 1960 on tour and in New York, she played an actress of an earlier era, Mrs. Patrick Campbell, in *Dear Liar*.

She received many honors during her long and distinguished career. Among them were the Freedom Medal, a medal from the American Academy of Arts and Letters, and eleven honorary doctorates from colleges and universities. She died 9 June 1974.

Katharine Cornell, 1898-1974

97. Katharine Cornell in the title role of George Bernard Shaw's *Candida*, by Eugene Speicher, 1926.

A native of New Jersey, Paul Robeson was born in Princeton on 9 April 1898 and was educated at Rutgers College, where he was selected twice as an All-American football player, and at Columbia University. He made his New York acting debut in *Simon the Cyrenian* at the Lafayette Theatre in 1921 and subsequently appeared as Jim in *Taboo* in New York and Blackpool, England. He was the personal choice of the playwright to act Brutus Jones in Eugene O'Neill's *The Emperor Jones* at the Provincetown Playhouse in 1924. London playgoers saw him in the part when he opened at the Ambassadors' Theatre in the English capital in the fall of 1925.

His first appearances in the musical theater came when he essayed the roles of Crown in Gershwin's *Porgy and Bess* in 1927 and Joe in Jerome Kern's *Show Boat* in London in 1928. During the 1929-1930 season he sang a number of concerts throughout Europe and also appeared in *The Emperor Jones* in Berlin. Robeson played Othello for the first time at London's Savoy Theatre on 19 May 1930. In 1936, again in London, he created the role of the liberator of Haiti in C. L. R. James's play *Toussaint L'Ouverture*. It opened at the Westminster Theatre in March, and London critics found Robeson's characterizations both sympathetic and important to the vitality of the play. Recognizing Paul Robeson's individuality as an artist, Charles Darwin, in *The Times* of 22 March 1936, wrote that "his appearance and voice entitle him to rules of his own."

He returned to the New York stage in the title role of *John Henry*, opening at the 44th Street Theatre on 10 January 1940. As a recitalist on the concert stage, he enjoyed phenomenal success. One concert in Chicago's Grant Park was attended by an estimated 150,000 persons.

On 19 October 1943 he played Othello for the first time in his native country in a Theatre Guild production at the Schubert Theatre. His Desdemona was Uta Hagen and his Iago, Jose Ferrer. Any valid criticism of Robeson's acting was buried under the controversy caused by the more than mildly racist critics who found a real black man in the role of Othello offensive. The play ran on Broadway, however, for 280 performances—a record for a Shakespearean production—and later toured.

During his travels in Europe, Paul Robeson had become more and more sympathetic to the aims and aspirations of the Soviet Union and, during a period of near hysterical anti-Communist feeling in the United States, was denied his passport in August of 1950. His professional activities were curtailed by his inability to travel abroad and by the inaccessibility of concert halls in this country. In 1958 he returned to Europe where he was named honorary professor at the Moscow State Conservatory of Music and where he played the title role in *Othello* at the Shakespeare Memorial Theatre, Stratford-upon-Avon, on 7 April 1959. He did not return to the United States until 1964—then to retirement in Philadelphia, where he died in March of 1976.

Paul Robeson's image as an actor was recorded by painters and sculptors as well as by photographers. A handsome head was sculpted by Jacob Epstein in 1928, and a quietly lyrical three-quarter-length portrait was painted by Edward Biberman in Los Angeles in 1947. A rough, but strong likeness of him in *Othello* was painted by Betsy Graves Reyneau in 1944 for the Harmon Foundation collection of portraits of eminent blacks. The portrait received more than a little attention in the American press when it was ordered removed from a traveling exhibition in Boston by Mayor John B. Hynes who differed with Robeson's political philosophy.

Paul Robeson, 1898-1976

98. Paul Robeson in the title role of Shakespeare's *Othello*, painted by Betsy Graves Reyneau shortly after the actor's appearance in the Theatre Guild's production of 1943.

99. Paul Robeson in the 1943 production of *Othello*, directed by
Margaret Webster.

Born in London, Gertrude Lawrence first appeared on stage in her native country at age nine as a dancer in a pantomime. She was first seen in the United States in New York when she came here with an *André Charlot's Revue* in 1924. She achieved her initial notable Broadway success as Kay in George and Ira Gershwin's *Oh Kay!* when it premiered at the Imperial Theatre in November of 1926. In 1928 she appeared with Clifton Webb in *Treasure Girl*, one of the Gershwins' few failures. As her star brightened over Broadway, she received critical acclaim for her appearance with Noël Coward in both *Private Lives*, which opened at the Times Square Theatre on 27 January 1931, and in *Tonight at 8:30*, one of the many hits of the extraordinary New York theater season of 1936-1937. In October of 1937 she began a long run in the role of Susan Trexel in Rachel Crother's *Susan and God* and was so successful in her part that one of New York's evangelists invited her to recite one of the play's more fervently religious speeches from his pulpit. Two seasons later she had another hit when she created the role of Lydia Kenyon in Sampson Raphaelson's *The Skylark*, which opened at the Morosco Theatre on 11 October 1939.

On 23 January 1941 she created the role of Liza Elliott in Kurt Weill's *Lady in the Dark* when it began its run at the Alvin Theatre. Challenged by the immediate success of comedian Danny Kaye, making his Broadway debut with her in the show, she gave what one of her critics termed "one of the remarkable virtuoso performances of our contemporary musical stage." To outdo Kaye she had reputedly asked Weill to compose a show-stopping number for her. The result was the raucous "Jenny." In December of 1945 she opened in New Haven in a revival of Shaw's *Pygmalion* which went on to a very successful New York engagement and a coast-to-coast tour. She saw in Anna Leonowens, the main character of Margaret Landon's novel *Anna and the King of Siam*, a superb vehicle for herself and persuaded Richard Rodgers and Oscar Hammerstein II to prepare a musical version for the New York stage. The result, *The King and I*, opened at the St. James Theatre on 29 March 1951 to critical acclaim. With Yul Brenner as her King of Siam, Gertrude Lawrence gave resplendent performances as Anna, English tutor to the King's children, until three weeks before her death on 6 September 1952.

At curtain time on the evening of the day of her funeral, the lights on the marquees of the theater districts in both New York and London were blacked out for two minutes in tribute to the departed star.

Gertrude Lawrence, 1898-1952

100. *Above:* Gertrude Lawrence and Yul Brynner in *The King and I*, 1951.
101. *Opposite page:* Gertrude Lawrence by Ben Ali Haggin, 1931.

Lotte Lenya was born in Vienna and made her debut as a performer at age six as a circus dancer. Later she trained professionally as a dancer in Zurich. Her Swiss teacher took her to Berlin where she appeared at first in any parts available to her. Discovered by Leopold Jenner, the manager of the Berlin State Theatre, she eventually made her debut at that renowned house.

In 1925 she met the composer Kurt Weill and they were married the following year. Weill soon was collaborating with Bertolt Brecht, and Lenya was given a principal singing role in their first venture together—*Die Kleine Mahagonny.* In August of 1928 Lenya created the role of Jenny in the Brecht-Weill *Die Dreigroschenoper,* an adaptation of John Gay's *The Begger's Opera.* Immediately controversial, the work was soon a hit throughout Europe and Lenya was a star.

In 1933, two years after the great director W. H. Pabst filmed *Die Dreigroschenoper,* Lenya and Weill wisely left Germany for France and two years later came to America. After acting in two short-lived productions, she retired from the stage. After her husband's death in 1950, she returned in a concert performance of *The Three Penny Opera,* singing the role she had created in Berlin. Four years later she sanctioned a fully-staged production in the English adaptation by Marc Blitzstein. On March 10, 1954, it opened at the Theatre de Lys, off Broadway, for a twelve week run. Again, Lenya sang the role of Jenny. *The New York Times* of the following day noted her "complete comprehension and mastery of the work." The run of the work was interrupted, but resumed again on September 20, 1955, and was to continue for more than six years. Souvenirs of the Theatre de Lys production were a Tony award for the show in 1956 and the Saul Bolasni portrait of Lenya in her famed role of Jenny.

When the Theatre de Lys production resumed, in September of 1955, the *Times* reviewer was even more effusive than the first time around. He wrote: "Miss Lenya is full of strength in this bitter role, bringing to it the vigor and pathos it embodies." An even more impassioned tribute was paid her by Harold C. Schonberg in *The New York Times* of August 2, 1958. Writing of a concert at New York's Lewisohn Stadium the night before, he penned a description of Lenya that has become classic: "She has a rasping voice that could sandpaper sandpaper, and half the time she does not even attempt to sing. But she can put into a song like 'Pirate Jenny' an intensity that becomes almost terrifying."

Lotte Lenya, 1900-

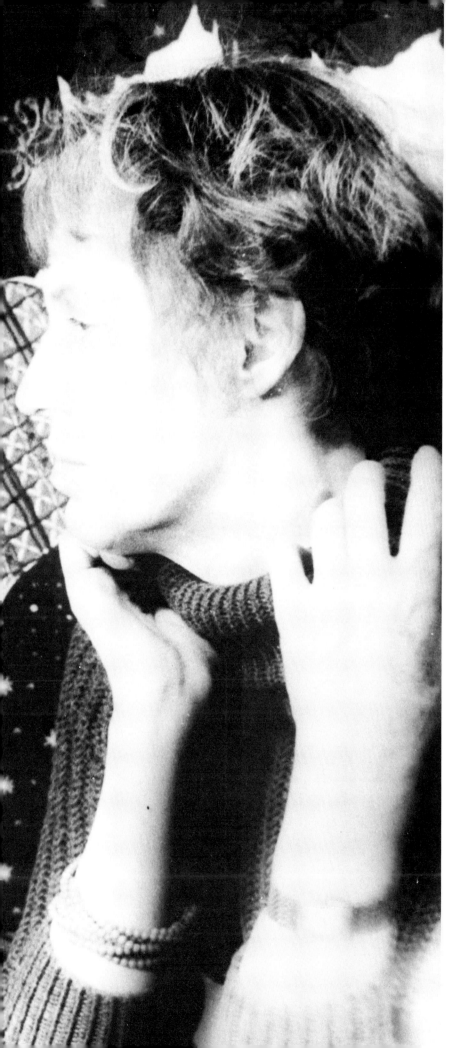

102. Lotte Lenya, by Carl Van Vechten, after 1935.

103. Lotte Lenya as Jenny in the 1954 production of *The Three Penny Opera*, by Saul Bolasni.

XV. Ethel Merman as Annie Oakley in Irving Berlin's *Annie Get Your Gun* by Rosemary Sloat, 1971. The portrait was painted from a life sitting and from photographs of the singer in her most noted role.

XVI. Martha Graham in the dance *Tragic Holiday* by Paul Meltsner, painted about 1940.

XVII. Regina Resnik as Klytämnestra in Richard Strauss's *Elektra* by Arbit Blatas, 1969. The singer is shown during the scene of confrontation between the Mycenaean queen and her daughter.

XVIII. *Top (left):* Self-portrait of Zero Mostel as John in Eugene Ionesco's *Rhinoceros*, 1960. As proud of himself as a painter as he was of being an actor, Mostel depicted his character at the moment that John begins to turn into a rhinoceros.

XIX. *Top (right):* Mae West by Salvador Dali, 1934. The whimsical surrealist painter shows the actress as a sitting room with open door.

XX. *Above:* Elvis Presley *(Elvis I and II)* by Andy Warhol, 1964.

Helen Hayes made her debut in 1905 on the stage of the National Theatre in her native Washington, D.C., where she was born on 10 October 1900. Her first role, a premonition of grander royalty to come later, was Prince Charles in a Columbia Players' production of *The Royal Family*.

Her New York debut was also made as a child actress when she opened as Little Mimi in *Old Dutch* at the Herald Square Theatre on 22 November 1909. One of her first successes as an adult was as Margaret in *Dear Brutus* which opened at the Empire Theatre on 23 December 1918. On 13 April 1925 Calvin Coolidge pushed a button in the nation's capital and gave the signal to raise the curtain on the first production in the Theatre Guild's new playhouse in New York. Appropriately enough, the heroine of that production of Shaw's *Caesar and Cleopatra* was Helen Hayes. She was again to star in the title role of a Theatre Guild production when Maxwell Anderson's *Mary of Scotland* opened in New York's Alvin Theatre on 27 November 1933.

The crown passed to her again when she created one of her most unforgettable roles at the opening of *Victoria Regina* on 26 December 1935. Her portrayal of the young and the aged Queen Victoria won her both a Drama League of New York award and the satisfaction of a successful tour. Her Broadway debut in a Shakespearean role occurred in another Theatre Guild production. It was the season of 1940-41, and the role was Viola in *Twelfth Night*. Somewhere along her busy and popularly received career, she was aptly dubbed "The First Lady of the American Theatre." A Helen Hayes Festival at the Falmouth Playhouse during the sumer of 1954, featuring Miss Hayes in re-creations of her original roles in *What Every Woman Knows*, *The Wisteria Tree*, and *Mary of Scotland*, was a testimony to her loyal following.

In 1960 and 1961 she was recognized as a valuable cultural property by the United States Department of State, which sent her on a tour of twenty-eight countries in Europe and South America. She was seen as Mrs. Antrobas in Thornton Wilder's *The Skin of Our Teeth* and as Amanda in Tennessee Williams's *The Glass Menagerie*. In the summer of 1962 she appeared with Maurice Evans in a program of readings from Shakespeare at the Stratford, Connecticut, American Shakespeare Festival and toured with the production during the season of 1962-1963.

Although her greatest moments have been on the New York stage, she has not forgotten her hometown. A long-time friend of the Drama Department of the Catholic University of America in Washington, D.C., she has supported its endeavors by appearing in its productions. Her last appearance with the University's Hartke Theatre was as Mary Tyrone in Eugene O'Neill's *Long Day's Journey into Night* in May, 1971. She announced it as her farewell to the American stage.

The major life portrait of Helen Hayes is the appropriately regal full-length by Furman Finck. Friends of Miss Hayes, who saw the artist's portrait of President Dwight D. Eisenhower in progress, persuaded her to sit for Finck. At the first sitting, immediate rapport was achieved between artist and subject when the two learned that they shared the same birthday.

Helen Hayes, 1900-

104. Helen Hayes and Michael Higgins in the 1971 Catholic University of America production of Eugene O'Neill's *Long Day's Journey into Night*.

Born in Pittsburgh, Martha Graham grew up in Santa Barbara, California. In 1916 she began studies at the Denishawn School of the Dance in Los Angeles and studied with both Ruth St. Denis and Ted Shawn. In 1919 she made her solo debut with the Denishawn Company as the female lead in Shawn's ballet with an Aztec theme, *Xochitl*. Four years later Miss Graham left Denishawn and was for a while a solo dancer with the *Greenwich Village Follies* and a member of the dance faculty at the Eastman School of Music.

On 18 April 1926 she appeared at the 48th Street Theatre in New York in a program of eighteen of her own choreographed works. A new era in American modern dance history was begun. Her first works reflected her Denishawn training, but later she broke with all the old traditions to create her own easily identifiable style. All the traditional steps and movements of classical ballet went out the window as Miss Graham evolved a new language of dance movement. She chose at times to work on a bare stage with only costumes and lights. She is credited with being the first choreographer of our time to use movable scenery, speech with dancing, and a chorus commenting upon the dance in progress. On 9 January 1930 *The New York Times* carried a headline "MARTHA GRAHAM GIVES DANCE WITHOUT MUSIC" when she introduced her *Project in Movement for a Divine Comedy* during a program at Maxine Elliot's Theatre.

Since 1926 Martha Graham has created well over 100 dances. Some, such as *Imperial Gesture*, and the unique *Lamentation*, which she first danced on 8 January 1930 in a seamless tubelike costume of knitted wool while seated on a bench, were commentaries on human experience. Others, such as *El Penitente*, created in August, 1940, at the Bennington Dance Festival, of which Miss Graham was a founder, and *Appalachian Spring*, which Miss Graham first danced in the Coolidge Auditorium of the Library of Congress on 30 October 1944, were derived from American themes. Still others, *Errand into the Maze*, *Clytemnestra*, *Alcestis*, and *Phaedra*, are obviously dancings of classical tales. In staging her creations she has collaborated with numerous notable contemporary composers, including Samuel Barber, Paul Hindemith, Gian-Carlo Menotti, Aaron Copland, and Norman Dello Joio. Isamu Noguchi has been the designer of handsome sets and costumes for her productions, notably *Frontier* (1935), *Appalachian Spring* (1944), *Night Journey* (1947), *Embattled Garden* (1958), and *Phaedra* (1962).

In 1962 Martha Graham and her company appeared in Israel on a tour sponsored by the State Department Cultural Exchange Program. For Tel-Aviv, Miss Graham created her *Legend of Judith* which she first danced there in the Habima Theatre on 25 October 1962. Since 1927 Miss Graham has been the head of the Martha Graham School of Contemporary Dance in New York.

Both the painter Edward Biberman and the sculptor Isamu Noguchi met the dancer through Ailes Gilmour, the sculptor's sister, who was a member of Graham's company. The Biberman painting was done from a series of life drawings made at recitals and rehearsals. Aside from the monumental corpus of photos of Martha Graham, the dancer is the subject of a series of paintings by Paul Meltsner. These seem all to have been done from photos.

Martha Graham, 1900-?

106. Martha Graham in recital, by Edward Biberman, 1930-31. Paul Meltsner's 1940 portrait of the dancer appears in color on p. 174.

When the portrait of cellist Gregor Piatigorsky by Wayman Adams won first prize at the Carnegie Institute exhibition in October of 1943, one of the art critics called it "savory, romantic." This could have been a capsule description of the career of the musician as well.

Sometimes called the "Russian Casals"—an appellation complimentary to both cellists—Piatigorsky was born in Ekaterinoslav, in the Ukraine, but fled his homeland in his late teens. In undertaking his self-exile in 1921, he was led across the border into Poland by smugglers, who, after performing their good deed of liberation, proceeded to rob Piatigorsky of money and clothes. Undaunted, he obtained a position as a member of the orchestra of the Warsaw Opera. Moving on to Berlin, he was eventually urged by the noted conductor Wilhelm Furtwängler to compete for a chair in the Berlin Philharmonic. His success in this endeavor was no surprise, and by 1923 he was the first cellist of that world-famed orchestra. In that same year he began to tour Europe as a soloist.

His American debut occurred in Oberlin, Ohio, on 5 November 1929. On 29 December, at a Sunday afternoon concert in New York's Carnegie Hall, he soloed for the first time with the New York Philharmonic. Hans Lange presided on the podium for Piatigorsky's performance of the Dvorak cello concerto. "Playing with emotional fire," as *The New York Times* put it, he thrilled his audience and the critics who proclaimed him "one of the most poetic and sensitive performers now before the public."

Gregor Piatigorsky toured both the Old and New Worlds for some twenty years and became an American citizen in 1942, the year that Wayman Adams painted him rehearsing. As if to strengthen the romantic chords of his life, he partook of both Worlds in his personal and professional lives. He became an American citizen, but he married the daughter of the very European Baron Édouard de Rothschild.

Some of his critics believed that Piatigorsky's playing brought about a renaissance of interest in the cello. One dictionary of musicians reported that his "technique is of the virtuoso order, but his interpretations are free from the eccentricities of the average virtuoso." From 1962 on he taught master classes in cello both in California and in Switzerland. Although he composed poetry in Russian, his biography, *Cellist,* was written in English.

On 20 May 1973, the Chamber Music Society of Lincoln Center sponsored a seventieth-birthday concert for Piatigorsky at Tully Hall. This extraordinary event featured seven other cellists, two pianists, and a soprano, all sharing the same stage without reported incident. After the music there was champagne and cookies for the entire audience. Writing of the bubbly event, Harold C. Schonberg praised Piatigorsky's playing, underscoring the "big line, the big ritard, the sentimental phrasing, the various expressive devices beloved of a previous generation." Piatigorsky made his last appearance at Philadelphia's Robin Hood Dell in June of 1975. He died at his Los Angeles home on 6 August 1976.

Gregor Piatigorsky, 1903-1976

109. Gregor Piatigorsky at practice, by Wayman Adams, 1942.

A relative of the famed British acting family, the Terrys, John Gielgud first appeared on stage as the Herald in Shakespeare's *Henry V* at London's Old Vic in November of 1921. His first appearance in the United States was at New York's Majestic Theatre on 19 January 1928 as the Grand Duke Alexander in *The Patriot*. His was a minor role in a minor play and the costume piece lasted only twelve performances.

When he returned to London, John Gielgud's reputation grew with his successive appearances on the stages of that city, and particularly with his own production of *Hamlet* in 1934 in which he took the title role. The production ran for 185 performances, a London theater record surpassed only by Sir Henry Irving's production sixty years earlier.

In 1936 Gielgud returned to New York with his *Hamlet* and opened at the Empire Theatre on 8 October. Judith Anderson was his Queen and Lillian Gish was his Ophelia in a production that most of the critics accepted as the outstanding *Hamlet* of their time. Brooks Atkinson, writing in *The New York Times* on 18 October, went so far in his enthusiasm as to give the actor the power of posthumous mind reading when he wrote that Gielgud "has not only the youth but also the temperament to understand Hamlet as Shakespeare imagined him." John Anderson in the *Evening Journal*, writing perhaps with unconscious chauvinism, found Gielgud's melancholy Dane second to that of John Barrymore, but admitted that some of his quieter passages were "nothing short of perfection." Gielgud's *Hamlet* ran for 132 performances, thirty-two more than that of Barrymore in 1922.

After World War II, Gielgud was much in evidence on the American stage. In the spring of 1947 alone, he appeared in New York in productions of Oscar Wilde's *The Importance of Being Earnest*, Congreve's *Love for Love*, and Robinson Jeffers's adaptation of *Medea* in which he played Jason opposite Judith Anderson in the title role. Late in December he opened at the National Theatre as Raskolnikoff in Rodney Acklan's version of Dostoevsky's *Crime and Punishment*. Brooks Atkinson considered Gielgud's characterization in this role one of his masterpieces. In 1950 he reappeared as Thomas Mendip in Christopher Fry's *The Lady's Not for Burning*. In acknowledgment of his services to the British stage, knighthood was conferred upon him by Queen Elizabeth II in the Coronation and Birthday Honors of 1953, and he became Sir John Gielgud.

In 1958 he toured Canada and the United States with *The Ages of Man* and then appeared on Broadway with this montage of Shakespearean passages. After a lengthy tour with the same production, which took him as far afield as Australia and New Zealand, Sir John opened with it again in New York in April of 1963. He was again seen on the New York stage during the season of 1970-1971 as one of the four-person cast of David Storey's *Home*. During the past two decades he has, with Sir Lawrence Olivier, become one of the outstanding character actors in international cinema.

Sir John Gielgud, 1904-

110. John Gielgud in the title role of Shakespeare's *Hamlet*, by Richmond Barthé, about 1936.

Outside of the silent cinema, there have been few American mimes of note in our century. The best known, undoubtedly, is Angna Enters. Born in New York on 28 April 1907, Miss Enters made her stage debut in her hometown at the Greenwich Village Theatre in the spring of 1924. The production was a program of dance and mime entitled *Compositions in Dance Form*, a recital in which she not only starred, but for which she had also designed the sets and costumes. With her program retitled *The Theatre of Angna Enters*, she began, several years later, to make annual tours of North America.

Miss Enters has been credited with coining the term "dance mime" to describe her unique contribution to the performing arts, and in this subtle medium she created, since her first performances in Greenwich Village, about 160 separate episodes and compositions. She has received her inspiration from many sources. A series of compositions were based on readings from Proust, one was inspired by the paintings of the eighteenth-century French artist Chardin, and others were based on individual and distinctive characters, such as her "Boy Cardinal" and "Queen of Heaven." On 25 January 1943 Angna Enters became the first person ever to stage a theatrical entertainment in New York's Metropolitan Museum of Art. Her work was entitled *Pagan Greece*, and for it she not only designed and executed her own costumes and choreography, but she composed the music and played all of the roles—some one dozen in number.

In 1952, while touring in England, she played two weeks of repertory at the Mercury Theatre, performed at Cambridge University, and was honored as the subject of a special program on BBC television. Whitney Bolton in the New York *Morning Telegraph* of 4 March 1959 penned as complimentary a description of a performer as any enthusiastic critic when he wrote that "Angna Enters is not solely a mime, nor uniquely a dancer. Her public performances combine all of these into an Enteresque concept no counterfeiter ever has been able to equal."

Miss Enters' paintings have been widely exhibited since her first one-woman exhibition in New York in 1933, and in October of 1963 a showing of her original designs for sets and costumes was a feature of the International Theatre Exhibition at Naples, Italy.

111, 112. *Left:* Angna Enters's own drawing of her mime character, the Queen of Heaven, 1971. *Opposite page:* Angna Enters, etching by Walt Kuhn, about 1925. The etching is signed by both subject and artist.

Angna Enters, 1907-

After graduation from St. Margaret's Academy in her native Waterbury, Connecticut, Lucia Chase studied acting at the Theatre Guild School, and dancing with several of the leading names in twentieth-century ballet and choreography—Mikhail Mordkin, Michel Fokine, Antony Tudor, Bronislava Nijinska, and others. In 1938 and 1939 she was a ballerina with the newly organized Mordkin Ballet. Miss Chase danced in *Giselle*, *La Fille Mal Gardée*, *The Goldfish*, and various other works under Mordkin's direction. In the autumn of 1939 the Mordkin Ballet became Ballet Theatre with Lucia Chase as founder-director.

With her company she created a number of notable dance roles. She was Minerva when Antony Tudor's ballet *The Judgment of Paris*, set to music from Kurt Weill's *The Three Penny Opera*, was first danced at New York's Center Theatre on 23 January 1940; she was "The Greedy One" at the premiere performance of Agnes de Mille's *Three Virgins and a Devil* on 11 February 1941. Later the same year, on 12 November, she danced Floretta in the American premiere of Fokine's *Bluebeard* in the Forty-fourth Street Theatre in New York. When Antony Tudor's *Pillar of Fire*, set to the music of Arnold Schönberg's *Verklärte Nacht*, was premiered by Ballet Theatre at the Metropolitan Opera House on 8 April 1942, Lucia Chase created the role of the Oldest Sister; on 29 November 1942 she was the first Pallas Athena in David Lachine's *Helen of Troy*. The following spring, on 6 April, Lucia Chase created the role of the Nurse in Antony Tudor's *Romeo and Juliet*. Although she did not create the role of the Stepmother in *Fall River Legend*, the ballet made from the story of Lizzie Borden to music by Morton Gould and choreography by Agnes de Mille, Miss Chase danced the role with her company for ten years.

In 1945 Ballet Theatre became the American Ballet Theatre and Lucia Chase became co-director with Oliver Smith. Under their directorship the company became one of the leading dance organizations in the United States. From August through December of 1950 the company, traveling as the American National Ballet Theatre, made its first European tour under the auspices of the State Department. Other foreign tours followed, the most notable being the September 1960 tour by which American Ballet Theatre became the first American dance company to appear in the Soviet Union.

Lucia Chase announced in January 1979 that she would retire as the company's artistic director on 1 September 1980.

Lucia Chase, 1907-

113. Lucia Chase in the ballet *Capriccioso*, by Boris Chaliapin, 1941.

The eighth of eleven children of an immigrant tailor, Benny Goodman was born in Chicago on 30 May 1909 and received his first clarinet and music lessons at the Kehelah Jacob Synagogue when he was ten. Other early musical training was received at the famous settlement house, Hull House, and he earned his first money as a musician when he was twelve. The following year he had his first union card, and at age fourteen he left school when he got a permanent job playing at Guyon's Paradise dance hall.

From 1925 until 1929 Benny Goodman played with Ben Pollack's band in Los Angeles, and made his first recorded solo with Pollack in December of 1926. In 1929 he was in New York playing in the orchestra pit at musicals and on the dance floor at college proms. In March of 1934 he formed his own band and opened at Billy Rose's Music Hall. A cross-country tour in the winter of the 1934-1935 season was a failure until the band hit Los Angeles. When dancers stopped dancing and crowded around the bandstand to listen to the soloists, the era of Swing had begun. In December of 1935 Benny Goodman held the first jazz concert in Chicago.

Upon his return to New York, more than 20,000 spectators paid admission to hear his first concert in the Paramount Theatre in March of 1937, and Benny Goodman was declared "The King of Swing." On 16 January 1938 the walls of New York's prim and proper yellow-brick music hall on 57th Street echoed jazz for the first time when Benny Goodman performed a concert in Carnegie Hall.

Shortly after the end of World War II, Benny Goodman broke up his band and did not assemble one again until early in 1956. In 1956 and 1957 he and his band made a most successful tour of Asia under the auspices of the Department of State, and in 1958 and 1959 he played at the Brussels World's Fair and toured western Europe. On Benny Goodman's fifty-third birthday, in 1962, he and his band began a tour of thirty-two concerts in the Soviet Union.

At home with the classics as well as with jazz, Benny Goodman commissioned a work for clarinet and violin from the composer Bela Bartok and has played and recorded both Mozart's *Concerto in A for Clarinet* and the same composer's *Quintet in A for Clarinet and Strings.*

Major concerts in recent years have included two in Carnegie Hall: In January of 1978 one was held to celebrate the fortieth anniversary of the first in that hall; the second, held on March 24, 1979, was performed as a salute to Mr. Goodman's seventieth birthday.

114. *Opposite page:* Benny Goodman, by René Bouché, 1960.

Benny Goodman, 1909-

A native of New York City's borough of Queens, Ethel Merman began her show business career in New York nightclubs and in vaudeville. One of her first engagements was at the Palace Theatre in the autumn of 1929 with a group that included Jimmy Durante. Her first appearance in a musical was as Kate Fothergill in George and Ira Gershwin's *Girl Crazy*, which opened at the Alvin Theatre on 14 October 1930. Her trumpet-voice renditions stopped the show and put her solidly in the theatrical headlines for the first time. When she sang her second feature number, "I Got Rhythm," a roaring audience demanded, and got, four encores. For that milestone performance George Gershwin himself conducted the orchestra, which included as instrumentalists Benny Goodman and Glenn Miller.

Not content with her vocal workout on the stage of the Alvin, Ethel Merman adjourned to the Central Park Casino every night after the closing of *Girl Crazy* to sing a late night show for its diamond-studded patronage. The following year found her opening at the Apollo Theatre on 14 September in *George White's Scandals* and then returning for a short while to vaudeville. Her next show, titled *Humpty Dumpty* when it flopped in Pittsburgh, was reworked into *Take a Chance* by its authors and made it to the Apollo by 26 November 1932, where it was a hit. More roles which Miss Merman herself called "hard-boiled Tessie types" followed between 1934 and 1943 when she created Reno Sweeney in *Anything Goes*, "Nails" O'Reilly Duquesne in Cole Porter's *Red, Hot and Blue*, Jeanette Adair in *Stars in Your Eyes*, Hattie Malony in *Panama Hattie*, and Blossom Hart in *Something for the Boys*.

In February of 1946 she went into rehearsal for the role which helped her break away into a new mood—Annie Oakley. *Annie Get Your Gun*, with music and lyrics by Irving Berlin, opened at the Imperial Theatre on 16 May 1946 after tryouts in New Haven, Boston, and Philadelphia. By New York opening night there was little doubt that Ethel Merman had created a role that would remain a classic in the annals of the American musical theater. *Annie Get Your Gun* graced the boards of the Imperial for 144 weeks.

On 12 October 1950 she opened again at the Imperial in another Irving Berlin show, *Call Me Madam*. In her role of Sally Adams, lady ambassador, a character based on the career of Perle Mesta, New York saw her for 644 performances; the rest of the country saw her when a motion picture version of the musical was released in 1953. In the same year she appeared with Mary Martin in the first two-hour television spectacular, a now legendary event that celebrated the fiftieth anniversary of the Ford Motor Company.

December of 1956 saw Miss Merman's opening in *Happy Hunting*, a musical that had a healthy run of 412 performances, and on 21 May 1959 she opened at the Broadway Theatre in *Gypsy*. Spiced with her impersonation of Rose, a hardboiled stage mother, the show ran for 702 performances in New York and finally closed on tour in St. Louis two and a half years later. In 1966, she again played Annie Oakley before sellout houses when *Annie Get Your Gun* was revived by the Music Theater of Lincoln Center.

In 1970 Ethel Merman was seen again on Broadway at the St. James Theatre when she assumed the role of Dolly Gallagher Levi in the record-setting Jerry Herman musical *Hello, Dolly!* It was between performances of this long-running show that Miss Merman was sketched for her first portrait, a portrait commissioned by a friend of the National Portrait Gallery so that the musical comedy star could be included in the museum's tribute to the opening of the John F. Kennedy Center for the Performing Arts. Since she had not created the role of Dolly, she asked instead to be depicted as Annie Oakley, her most famous characterization and a fitting symbol of her vital individualism.

Ethel Merman, 1909-

115. Ethel Merman as Annie Oakley in Irving Berlin's *Annie Get
Your Gun*, by Rosemarie Sloat, 1971. This portrait appears in color
on p. 173.

116, 117. *Left:* Ethel Merman and Bert Lahr in *Du Barry Was a Lady,* 1939. *Above:* The famous musical-comedy star singing "Blow, Gabriel, Blow" in *Anything Goes,* 1934.

By the time Alicia Markova made her dance debut in the United States in the autumn of 1938, she had been onstage for fourteen years and had secured an enviable reputation in her native England. She had been accepted in Sergei Diaghilev's Ballets Russes at age fourteen and had remained with that company until the impresario's death in 1929. With that company she created the title role in George Balanchine's *Le Rossignol* in 1926. Moving on to London's Ballet Rambert, she created leading roles in *La Peri, Les Masques,* and *Mephisto Valse,* all choreographed by Frederick Ashton. In April of 1931 she also created the Polka in Ashton's *Façade,* which he choreographed to music by William Walton. In 1933 she became the first prima ballerina of the Vic-Wells (now Royal) Ballet. While with that company, she became the first English ballerina to dance the title role in *Giselle* and the dual roles of Odette and Odile in a full-length production of Tchaikovsky's *Swan Lake.* With Anton Dolin she organized the Markova-Dolin Company and danced as its prima ballerina, from 1935 until 1938. In that year she became a ballerina in the René Blum-Leonide Massine Ballet Russe de Monte Carlo. When she danced the title role in *Giselle* in the company's first New York season in 1938, she became an immediate favorite of American audiences, whose understanding of ballet she greatly influenced.

She was a ballerina with the Ballet (now American Ballet) Theatre from 1941 until 1944 and again in the season of 1945-1946. For the Ballet Theatre she created the important role of Juliet in Anthony Tudor's *Romeo and Juliet,* set to music of Frederick Delius. The ballet, with decor by Eugene Berman, was premiered at the Metropolitan Opera House in New York on 6 April 1943 in unfinished form and four days later was given in full. In the season of 1945-1946 Miss Markova formed a new Markova-Dolin Company and took it on tour of the United States.

In the spring and summer of 1947 her company toured in Mexico and Central America. In 1948 she toured the Philippines with Anton Dolin and the following year South Africa. Returning to London, Alicia Markova was co-founder with Anton Dolin of the London Festival Ballet in 1950-1951 and was its prima ballerina. After twelve years as a guest dancer with leading companies all over the world, Miss Markova danced for the last time with the London Festival Ballet in 1962. She announced her retirement on 1 January 1963 and three months later became the director of the Metropolitan Opera Ballet.

Her influence in the old yellow-brick opera house on Broadway was not slight. On 15 November 1964 she presented the Metropolitan Opera Ballet in *Les Sylphides,* and, as a result of its successful reception by the administration and public, a ballet evening was scheduled at the opera house for 11 April 1965. It was only the second time in the eighty-year history of the Opera that such an evening had been scheduled. Of more widespread influence was certainly Miss Markova's direction of the Metropolitan Ballet Studio which performed before thousands of public school children in New York.

For her importance in ballet in Great Britain, she was made a Commander of the Order of the British Empire in 1960 and a Dame of the Order of the British Empire in 1963.

Alicia Markova, 1910-

118. Alicia Markova as Odette
in Tchaikovsky's *Swan Lake*, by
Boris Chaliapin, 1941.

Zero Mostel, born in Brooklyn on 28 February 1915, made his first public theatrical appearances in Greenwich Village club reviews. Moving uptown, he made his Broadway debut in April of 1942 at the 44th Street Theatre. The production was a review called *Keep 'Em Laughing*. He was Hamilton Peachum in *Beggar's Holiday* at the Broadway Theatre late in 1946 and Glubb in *Flight into Egypt* at the Music Box early in 1952. In July of the same year he played in his own adaptation of Molière's *The Imaginary Invalid* at the Brattle Theatre in Cambridge, Massachusetts. On 5 June 1958, at the Rooftop Theatre, he opened as Leopold Bloom in *Ulysses in Nighttown*. For his performance, Zero Mostel won an "Obie" awarded by *The Village Voice* for the best off-Broadway performance.

Another success followed with the opening of a production of Eugene Ionesco's *Rhinoceros* at the Longacre Theatre on 9 January 1961. Walter Kerr's review in the *Herald Tribune* humorously echoed the acclaim that all the New York critics lavished on Mostel for his reading of the part of John, and gave a vivid description of the great scene of his metamorphosis into the wild animal: "'Rhinoceros' is an entertainment in which an extremely talented rhinoceros plays Zero Mostel. . . . The shoulders lift, the head juts forward, one foot begins to beat the earth with such native majesty that dust—real dust—begins to rise like the after-veil that seems to accompany a safari." For this characterization, Mostel was the recipient of a "Tony."

A third award, another "Tony," was in the not-too-distant future when *A Funny Thing Happened on the Way to the Forum* opened at the Alvin Theatre on 8 May 1962 with Zero Mostel as the freedom-seeking slave Pseudolus. In the autumn of 1964 Mostel created the role of Tevye at the opening of *Fiddler on the Roof*, which by this time has become a Broadway monument. Like his ancestor in American comedy, Joseph Jefferson, Zero Mostel was a painter, and many of his offstage hours were spent in his studio in mid-Manhattan, where his work was as profilic as his wisecracks. When preparing a role, Zero Mostel often painted himself as the character he was about to play. His self-portraits as Bloom, John, and Tevye are unique artistic documents of his stage career.

He died in Philadelphia in November of 1977 while preparing his role as Shylock in *The Merchant*, an adaptation of Shakespeare's *The Merchant of Venice*.

Zero Mostel, 1915-1977

119, 120. *Opposite page:* Zero Mostel and Eli Wallach in Eugene
Ionesco's *Rhinoceros*, caricature by Al Hirschfeld, 1960. *Above:* Zero
Mostel's self-portrait as John in *Rhinoceros*, 1960. The actor has
shown himself turning into the raging beast. This self-portrait appears in color on p. 176.

Born in Brooklyn, Lena Horne worked her way into show business the hard way, as a member of a night club chorus line. In the Fall of 1933 she started working at the Cotton Club in Harlem. It was there that she first began singing small solos. In 1935 and 1936 she toured with Noble Sissle's Society Orchestra, a noted black band of the period. It was the first black orchestra to play the roof of the Ritz-Carlton in New York, even if, as Miss Horne puts it with appropriate acidity, they "had to come in through the kitchen door." In 1937 she married, and, after a hiatus of two years, she was back again as a band vocalist when she was hired by Charlie Barnet.

Theater people began to take notice of her, and it wasn't long before she was engaged by New York's popular nightspot, Cafe Society Downtown. During this same time she was recorded by RCA-Victor, and she also began to be heard on New York radio.

In 1942 she was appearing at Hollywood's Little Troc and Mocambo when the motion picture industry took notice of her vocal talent and her physical beauty. A bit part followed in *Panama Hattie* and then a larger role in the 1943 all-black musicals *Cabin in the Sky* and *Stormy Weather*. In the Fall of 1942, she returned to New York for more cabaret appearances. While appearing at the Savoy-Plaza, she was interviewed by the *New York Post*. Aside from a bit of pertinent wartime gossip—"Humphrey Bogart is my air-raid warden"—readers were allowed a first glimpse of an engaging personality. When asked how many songs she sang during a night at the Savoy-Plaza's Cafe Lounge, she replied, "As many as they are polite enough to let me." In 1947 she was off across the Atlantic for her first appearances in European clubs. In 1950 she played London's famous Palladium for the first time. Later she would return there for a command performance before Queen Elizabeth II.

After she returned to the United States, her career became somewhat frozen, a situation perhaps best summed up by her own comment that she "played the Sands for a decade." She was frequently a headliner at the famed Las Vegas watering spot. Although she was temporarily red-listed during the communist-scare era, work came to her again, and she was soon a popular guest on the TV shows hosted by Ed Sullivan, Steve Allen, and Perry Como.

Although she had appeared in a bit part in the short-lived 1934 Broadway show *Dance with Your Gods*, it was not until 1957 that she could count herself as much a star on the Great White Way as she was on the club circuit. On October 31, 1957, she opened as Savanna in the musical *Jamaica*. The following day John Chapman in *The Daily News* obviously considered Lena Horne *the* show when he observed that "'Jamaica' Has Horne, Needs Plot." The *Times's* critic, Brooks Atkinson noted that "For a number of years she has been hiding her talent in supper clubs. It is out in the open now."

121. *Opposite page:* Lena Horne on stage, by Edward Biberman, 1947.

Lena Horne, 1917-

Although born at New York's Flower Hospital at Fifth Avenue and 106th Street on 23 December 1923, Maria Callas began her professional career in Greece. Taken there in 1936 by her mother, she was enrolled a year later as a student at the National Conservatory in Athens. Her first stage appearance was in a student production of *Cavalleria rusticana* in 1938. Her debut in the title role of Puccini's *Tosca* with the Athens Opera in July of 1942 was the highlight of her early European career.

She returned to New York for two years in 1945, but, finding little impetus here for a career in opera, she returned to Europe where she made her Italian debut in August of 1947 in the Arena of Verona. The opera was *La Gioconda*; the reviews were polite, but not overly enthusiastic. Then things began to happen: An Isolde and Turandot at La Fenice in Venice; another Isolde in Genoa; Elvira in Bellini's *I Puritani*, again at La Fenice. On 12 April 1950 she made her debut at the most sacred of all Italian shrines of opera, Milan's La Scala. The reviews of her Aïda that night praised her acting more than her singing. She became known as a singer who could sing anything, especially for the fiendishly difficult roles of the bel canto repertory. Operas of the first half of the nineteenth century which had not been heard for decades were revived for her. She was compared with Maria Malibran, Guiditta Pasta, and with other singers who are legends in the annals of operatic performance. So popular had she become at La Scala that she was chosen to sing in the opening-night opera of all seasons but one from 1951 to 1955.

On 1 November 1954 she returned in triumph to the United States, singing the title role of Bellini's *Norma* with the Lyric Opera of Chicago. The response by press and by public indicated that a new era in operatic history in America had begun. She made her Metropolitan Opera debut, again as the ill-fated Celtic priestess, on 29 October 1956. A month later New York saw the full force of her dramatic ability in performances of Puccini's *Tosca*. In 1958 Dallas audiences rose to cheer her interpretation of the vengeful heroine of Luigi Cherubini's *Medea*, an opera resurrected from the obscurity of time by her presence on the operatic stage.

As she achieved celebrity, yellow journalism's gossip columns constantly reported the fortunes and misfortunes of her private life, while the music critics praised her one-woman act of resurrecting a golden age of opera. She did not create any new roles to serve as examples for future singers, but she re-created the leading soprano roles in the florid operas of the past century, and brought life into lyric characters who too often appeared as lifeless animated cutouts. "La Divina," as her more fervent admirers called her, added a new aspect to her career when, in 1970, she began a series of teaching lectures at New York's Juilliard School of Music.

In 1974 she returned to the concert stage for a series of recitals with Giuseppe De Stephano. She sang for the last time in public in Japan and died in Paris on September 16, 1977.

Maria Callas, 1923-1977

122. Maria Callas, by Henry Koerner, 1956.

Regina Resnik made her first appearances on stage in student productions of Gilbert and Sullivan operettas at New York's Hunter College. In 1942 she was engaged by the New York City Opera where she made her debut as Lady Macbeth in Verdi's operatic version of Shakespeare's famous tragedy. The following year she entered the Metropolitan Opera Auditions of the Air and progressed to the finals when she dropped out to sing several performances of Wagner in Mexico City. In 1944 she again entered the Auditions, was the only woman finalist, and received a contract from the Metropolitan Opera. She was scheduled to make her debut with that company as Santuzza in *Cavalleria rusticana*, but the indisposition of another soprano found her making her debut on 6 December 1944 as Leonora in Giuseppe Verdi's *Il Trovatore* on twenty-four hours' notice and without either orchestral or stage rehearsal.

Until 1953 she sang the more or less standard soprano roles of the repertoire, ranging from Rosalinde in *Die Fledermaus* to Sieglinde in *Die Walküre*, a role which she sang in 1953 at that year's Bayreuth Festival. After adding several mezzo-soprano parts to her repertory—the title role in *Carmen*, Venus in *Tannhäuser*, and the Princess Eboli in Verdi's *Don Carlo*—she decided about 1955 to forsake the soprano range and to be a mezzo-soprano. It is in this lower range that she has achieved her most notable success.

In the fall of 1957 Regina Resnik made her Covent Garden debut as Carmen. The appreciative reviews by the English critics were among the first she received over the years as one of the more popular interpreters of this demanding role. The following year she returned to the same opera house to sing Marina in the Russian-language production of *Boris Godunov* that opened the 1958-1959 season. On 15 January 1958 she created the role of the Old Baroness in the Metropolitan Opera world premiere of Samuel Barber's *Vanessa*. She has become especially noted for her singing and acting of the tortured, guilt-ridden Klytämnestra in Richard Strauss's *Elektra*. After she portrayed the Theban queen at the Metropolitan in the spring of 1971, a critic of *The New York Times* called it "a role she has made her own."

Also in the spring of 1971 she began a career as a director of opera when she teamed with artist Arbit Blatas to design and direct a production of *Carmen* for the Hamburg Opera and one of *Elektra* for the Teatro La Fenice in Venice. After one performance in late June, the audience awarded *Carmen* an astounding fifty-three curtain calls.

In 1972 Miss Resnik starred as Claire Zachanassian in the American premiere of Gottfried von Einem's operatic adaptation of the Friedrich Dürrenmatt play, *The Visit*. The production, staged by Francis Ford Coppola, was a highlight of the fiftieth anniversary season of the San Francisco Opera. With Arbit Blatas, Miss Resnik has shared the chores of opera design and production as far afield as Warsaw, Poland, Strasbourg, France, and Sydney, Australia.

Regina Resnik, 1921-

123, 124. Regina Resnik as Klytämnestra in Richard Strauss's *Elektra*, by Arbit Blatas, 1969. This portrait appears in color on p. 175. *Overleaf*: Regina Resnik on stage at the Metropolitan Opera as the old countess in Tchaikovsky's *Pique Dame, 1966*.

Marilyn Horne was seven years old when she began her formal voice training in Buffalo, New York, not far from her hometown of Bradford, Pennsylvania, where she was born in 1934. In 1945 her family moved to California, and it was there that she began her professional career as a singer with the Roger Wagner Chorale. After further voice study at the University of Southern California, she sang her first solo concerts in Los Angeles and made her operatic debut in 1954 in a Los Angeles Opera Guild production of Bedrich Smetana's *The Bartered Bride*. The following year she was the singing voice of Dorothy Dandridge on the soundtrack of the movie *Carmen Jones*. A European debut at the 1956 Venice Biennale was followed by an apprenticeship with the local opera company in Gelsenkirchen, Germany.

Returning to the United States in 1960, she made her San Francisco Opera debut as Marie in Alban Berg's *Wozzeck* in the autumn of that yera, and in February of 1961 Miss Horne made her New York operatic debut at Carnegie Hall in a concert performance of Bellini's *Beatrice di Tenda*. The performance was also the occasion of the New York debut of the Australian soprano Joan Sutherland, and although *The New York Times* was later to heap praise on the joint appearances by the two ladies, it did not mention Marilyn Horne in its review of the *Beatrice*.

Her Covent Garden debut, once again as Marie in *Wozzeck*, was decidedly more successful, and when she returned to Carnegie Hall for another American Opera Society production in 1964— Rossini's *Semiramide*—audiences screamed and critics raved. In 1969 Milan's La Scala revived Rossini's *Assedio di Corinto* with a largely American cast. Marilyn Horne's bravura singing of a notoriously difficult twenty-four-and-a-half minute scena was understandably a high point of the performance.

On Tuesday 3 March 1970 she made her debut at the Metropolitan Opera House in a new production of Bellini's *Norma*. Singing Adalgisa to the Norma of her friend Joan Sutherland, she was loudly applauded the moment she appeared on stage—even before she had sung a note. The press did anything but pass over her performance this time. The following Thursday, the *Times's* Harold Schonberg was moved to superlatives describing her solo passages and her duets with Miss Sutherland. *Time* of 16 March punned that "Horne, making one of the greatest Met debuts, showed a vocal reach and a richness that exceeded nearly anybody's gasp."

In the season of 1970-1971, the Lyric Opera of Chicago staged Rossini's *L'Italiana in Algeri* as a showcase for her particular talent, and she appeared as Rosina in the same composer's *Il Barbiere de Siviglia* at the Met. On 24 September 1971 she joined forces again with Joan Sutherland for an evening of blood-and-thunder bel canto when Chicago opened its season with a new production of Rossini's *Semiramide*.

A reprieve from the Italian bel canto repertory came with a triumphant Carmen at the Met, opening the 1972-1973 season. On 15 October 1975 she was the Rinaldo in the American stage premiere of the Handel work presented by the Houston Grand opera. In January of 1977 she was back at the Met for that company's first performance of Meyerbeer's *Le Prophete* in fifty years. *The New York Times* reviewer found that her singing made her "the vocal star of the evening." In November 1977 she was again a big and bright star deep in the heart of Texas. This time she was Romeo in the Dallas Civic Opera production of a hybrid *I Capeletti ed I Montecci* that utilized portions of versions by both Bellini and Vaccaj. Her last new role at the Met has been that of the Princess Eboli in Verdi's *Don Carlo*, sung there for the first time on 5 February 1979.

Marilyn Horne, 1934-

125, 126. *Opposite page:* Marilyn Horne on the stage of the Metropolitan Opera as the Princess Eboli in Verdi's Don Carlo, 1979. *Above:* Marilyn Horne as Adelgisa in Bellini's *Norma*, by John Foote, 1971. The portrait was painted to commemorate the mezzo-soprano's Metropolitan Opera debut.

The art critic David Bourdon once characterized Andy Warhol as "a maker of commemorative icons." How appropriate, then, that he should have executed at least seventeen images of Elvis Presley in the years 1962 through 1964. By the '60s Presley had become the highest paid performer in the history of show business, and he was well on his way to being a cult figure for his fans. Warhol's icons, with names like *Red Elvis*, *Double Elvis*, and *Elvis Diptych I and II*, were a fitting flashy homage to rock 'n' roll's first real star. All the "portraits" were based upon a publicity photo of the singer.

Elvis Presley was born in Tupelo, Mississippi, and moved to Memphis in 1949. He had gotten his first guitar at about age twelve and made his first record—for his mother—in 1953. A chance hearing of this personal cutting by a president of a record company led to his first contract and first commercial records. Elvis was on his way to stardom.

Within a few years he had evolved his very own personal style of performing and was attracting a following of fans. On his first network television appearance, he sang *Heartbreak Hotel* and had a best-selling record several weeks later. His own personal style, however, was physical as well as vocal and was marked by a pronounced gyrating of his hips. The TV cameras of the '50s showed him only

Elvis Presley, 1935-1977

from the waist up. His personal appearances earned him the nickname "Elvis the Pelvis" and the taunts of all the moralists in the country.

In 1957 Presley made the first of twenty-eight films, including one said to have been made in fifteen days for which he supposedly received one million dollars. In 1958 he was drafted into the U.S. Army for two years. When he returned from active duty, he curtailed his personal appearances so that from the early '60s on he appeared only in films. After a decade, he began to appear in nightclubs.

He mellowed toward the end of his career as he began to be revered as a grandfather of rock. He always had a loyal following of fans, from the teenagers who screamed when he sang *Hound Dog* to the matrons who sighed when he crooned *Love Me Tender*. In fact, the teenagers of 1956 had become the matrons of 1976. A potent force on the American musical scene until the advent of British rock groups, Elvis Presley was taken more seriously as a musician toward the end of his career. He died at his Tennessee home on August 15, 1977, having burned himself out by the age of forty-two.

127. Elvis Presley (Elvis I and II), by Andy Warhol, 1964. This portrait appears in color on p. 176.

Joan Baez was born on Staten Island, New York, on 9 January 1941, grew up in towns from coast to coast, and bought her first guitar from a mail-order house when she was in high school in Palo Alto, California. After high school, her family moved to Boston and she began her professional career there, singing in the coffeehouses in the university areas on both sides of the Charles River. She hit the big time when she appeared at the 1959 Folk Festival at Newport, Rhode Island. Recording companies vied for her favors, and she finally signed a contract with the stipulation that she only be required one album a year. Soon after her recording debut, she became the first folk musician ever to have an album on the charts of best sellers. By November of 1962, three of her albums achieved the same degree of commercial prominence at the same time. On 23 November 1967, her portrait was featured on the cover of *Time*, which called her the "tangible sibyl" of folk music in America.

Her repertory of the folk singers' standard bag of old English and Scottish songs was augmented with works by the young Bob Dylan and with increasing numbers of songs of protest, as her professional engagements became a sounding board for her personal views on the turbulent American scene in the late '60s. Musically, she achieved a style which was copied by many aspiring young folk singers. In acquiescence to a growing taste for electric rock, she is said to have made one album in that mood in 1967, but it was never released. In the same year she became increasingly involved in the activities of a school for nonviolence, and her concert appearances became fewer in number.

In the late summer of 1967, Joan Baez was denied the use of Constitution Hall in Washington, D.C., because of her outspoken views against the war in Southeast Asia and her refusal to pay income tax. Thereupon she received permission from the Department of the Interior to give a free concert on the grounds of the Washington Monument. She performed on the evening of 14 August 1967 before a crowd variously estimated at from 10,000 to 30,000 people. Carl Bernstein, reporting in the *Washington Post* the following morning, called the concert a "monumental personal and musical triumph" for Joan Baez.

128. Opposite page: Joan Baez, by Russell Hoban, 1962.

Joan Baez, 1941-

Born in Seattle 27 November 1945, Jimi Hendrix started playing the electric guitar at the age of twelve. After serving with the United States Army, he played in almost fifty rock and roll groups from the West Coast to Greenwich Village before going to England in 1966. There, backed up by bass and drum, the Jimi Hendrix Experience conquered the popular music scene in about six months' time. Readers of the English pop-music papers voted him the world's "top musician."

The Experience made its first appearance in the United States at the Monterey Pop Festival in June of 1967. The actions of Jimi Hendrix on stage were as violent as his music—one of his biographers called him a "psychedelic hootchie-kootchie man"—and even less subtly erotic. Later in the summer of 1967 the Experience started on its first American tour as a backup group to The Monkees. The hue and cry that went up after Hendrix's exhibition of guitar nuzzling and pelvic thrusts forced the Experience off the remainder of the Monkees' tour. The resultant publicity, his showmanship, and his musicianship all combined to put Jimi Hendrix right at the top with the leading rock groups—the Beatles and the Rolling Stones—and with Bob Dylan within a year's time.

One of his more monumental musical performances was his playing of "The Star-Spangled Banner" at the musical orgy held at Woodstock, New York, in August of 1969. Later that year the Experience broke up, but Jimi Hendrix reappeared at New York's Fillmore East on New Year's Eve with a new group, the Band of Gypsies, which was in turn dissolved only a few weeks later.

In the spring of 1970 the Experience was re-formed. They had just finished a tour of Europe and had performed in the late summer Isle of Wight Festival when Jimi Hendrix died of an overdose of barbituates in London on 18 September 1970.

129. *Opposite page:* Jimi Hendrix, as modeled posthumously by Jack Gregory in 1971.

Jimi Hendrix, 1945-1970

Credits

1. Library of Congress.   2. Ibid.   3. National Portrait Gallery, Smithsonian Institution. Photo: Eugene Mantie.   4. Courtesy of The Walter Hampden-Edwin Booth Theatre Collection and Library at The Players. Photo: Geoffrey Clements.   5. Ibid.   6. Library of Congress.   7. Museum of the City of New York, Theatre and Music Collection.   8. The New-York Historical Society, New York City.   9. Honolulu Academy of Arts.   10. Colonial Williamsburg Foundation.   11. Pennsylvania Academy of the Fine Arts.   12. Historical Society of York County. Photo: Jim Hayman.   13. Ibid.   14. Courtesy of the Players. Photo: Eugene Mantie.   15. Corcoran Gallery of Art, Anna E. Clark Fund.   16. Metropolitan Museum of Art, Rogers Fund, 1906.   17. Museum of the City of New York, Theatre and Music Collection.   18. Courtesy of The Players. Photo: Geoffrey Clements.   19. The New York Public Library, Cia Fornaroli Collection, Dance Collection.   20. National Portrait Gallery, London.   21. Harvard Theatre Collection.   22. Ibid.   23. The Edwin Forrest Home. Photo: Eugene Mantie.   24. Music Division, Library of Congress.   25. Photo: Eugene Mantie.   26. National Portrait Gallery, Smithsonian Institution. Photo: Eugene Mantie.   27. Pennsylvania Academy of the Fine Arts.   28. Indianapolis Museum of Art, gift of Mrs. John E. Fehsenfeld.

29. Photo: Eugene Mantie.   30. Library of Congress, Division of Prints and Photographs.   31. Haydn Museum, Eisenstadt, Austria. Photo: Eugene Mantie.   32. National Portrait Gallery, Smithsonian Institution. Photo: Eugene Mantie.   33. Ibid.   34. Chicago Historical Society. Photo: Eugene Mantie.   35. Library of Congress, Division of Prints and Photographs.   36. Ibid.   37. National Portrait Gallery, London.   38. The New-York Historical Society, New York City.   39. Photo: Eugene Mantie.   40. Dance Collection, The New York Public Library.   41. Courtesy of Parmenia Migel Ekstrom.   42. Courtesy of the Walter Hampden-Edwin Booth Theatre Collection and Library at The Players. Photo: Eugene Mantie.   43. Ibid. Photo: Geoffrey Clements.   44. Museum of the City of New York, Theatre and Music Collection.   45. The New-York Historical Society, New York City.   46. Ibid.   47. Ibid.   48. McLellan Lincoln Collection, Brown University.   49. Harvard Theatre Collection.   50. National Portrait Gallery, Smithsonian Institution.   51. Museum of the City of New York, Theatre and Music Collection.   52. National Portrait Gallery, Smithsonian Institution. Photo: Eugene Mantie.   53. Courtesy of Gordon Colket. Photo: Eugene Mantie.   54. The Phillips Collection.   55. Courtesy of Lillian Nassau.   56. Library of Congress, Division of Prints and

Photographs.   57. National Gallery of Art, Rosenwald Collection.   58. National Portrait Gallery, Smithsonian Institution; lent by The National Gallery of Art. Photo: Eugene Mantie.   59. Library of Congress, Division of Prints and Photographs.   60. National Portrait Gallery, Smithsonian Institution. Photo: Eugene Mantie.   61. Metropolitan Museum of Art, Gift of Sir William Van Horne, 1906.   62. Stephens College.   63. The Metropolitan Museum of Art.   64. Metropolitan Opera Association. Photo: courtesy of Opera News.   65. Ibid. Photo: Eugene Mantie.   66. Library of Congress, Division of Prints and Photographs.   67. Courtesy of the artist.   68. National Portrait Gallery, Smithsonian Institution. Photo: Eugene Mantie.   69. Steinway & Sons. Photo: Geoffrey Clements.   70. National Portrait Gallery, Smithsonian Institution. Photo: Eugene Mantie.   71. Courtesy of John Christian.   72. The Pennsylvania Academy of the Fine Arts.   73. Hirshhorn Museum and Sculpture Garden, Smithsonian Institution.   74. National Portrait Gallery, Smithsonian Institution. Photo: Eugene Mantie.   75. Ibid.   76. Museum of the City of New York, Theatre and Music Collection.   77. Ibid.   78. Ibid.   79. Courtesy of Mr. and Mrs. Val Lewton. Photo: Eugene Mantie.   80. National Portrait Gallery, Smithsonian Institution. Photo: Eugene Mantie.   81. Ibid.

222

82. Photo: Peter Juley & Sons Collection, National Collection of Fine Arts, Smithsonian Institution. Courtesy of the Malvina Hoffman Estate. 83. Museum of the City of New York, Theatre and Music Collection. 84. Ibid. 85. National Portrait Gallery, Smithsonian Institution. Photo: Eugene Mantie. 86. Library of Congress, Music Division. 87. Museum of the City of New York, Theatre and Music Collection. 88. Library of Congress, Division of Prints and Photographs. 89. Courtesy of Count Cyril McCormack. Photo: Eugene Mantie. 90. Museum of Fine Arts, Boston. 91. Metropolitan Opera Association. 92. Collection of Whitney Museum of American Art. 93. Courtesy of Lynn Fontanne. Photo: C. Richard Eells. 94. Museum of the City of New York, Theatre and Music Collection. 95. Privately owned. Photo: courtesy of Hirschl and Adler Galleries. 96. Museum of the City of New York, Theatre and Music Collection. 97. Albright-Knox Gallery. 98. National Portrait Gallery, Smithsonian Institution. 99. Museum of the City of New York, Theatre and Music Collection. 100. Ibid. 101. Ibid. 102. Ibid. 103. National Portrait Gallery, Smithsonian Institution. Photo: Eugene Mantie. 104. Photo: courtesy of the Speech and Drama Department, Catholic University of America. 105. National Portrait Gallery, Smithsonian Institution. 106. Courtesy of the artist. 107. American Shakespeare Festival Theatre. Photo: Joseph Szaszfai. 108. National Portrait Gallery, Smithsonian Institution. 109. Indianapolis Museum of Art. Photo: Robert Wallace. 110. American Shakespeare Festival Theatre. Photo: Joseph Szaszfai. 111. Privately owned. Photo: Eugene Mantie. 112. National Portrait Gallery, Smithsonian Institution. Photo: Eugene Mantie. 113. Courtesy of the artist. 114. Courtesy of Benny Goodman. 115. National Portrait Gallery, Smithsonian Institution. Photo: Eugene Mantie. 116. Museum of the City of New York, Theatre and Music Collection. 117. Ibid. 118. Courtesy of the artist. 119. Courtesy of Anne Jackson and Eli Wallach. 120. Courtesy of Kathryn Mostel. Photo: Eugene Mantie. 121. Courtesy of the artist. 122. National Portrait Gallery, Smithsonian Institution. Copyright © 1956 Time Inc. All rights reserved. Photo: Eugene Mantie. 123. Courtesy of Regina Resnik and Arbit Blatas. Photo: Eugene Mantie. 124. Photo: Louis Melancon. 125. Author's Collection. 126. Privately owned. Photo: Eugene Mantie. 127. Art Gallery of Ontario, Toronto; gift of the Women's Committee Fund, 1966. 128. National Portrait Gallery, Smithsonian Institution. Copyright © 1969 Time Inc. All rights reserved. Photo: Eugene Mantie. 129. Originally appeared in *Playboy* Magazine; copyright © 1971 by Playboy.

I. Colonial Williamsburg Foundation. II. Pennsylvania Academy of the Fine Arts. III. National Portrait Gallery, Smithsonian Institution. Photo: Eugene Mantie. IV. Corcoran Gallery of Art, Anna E. Clark Fund. V. Royal College of Music, London. VI. Library of Congress, Music Division. VII. National Portrait Gallery, Smithsonian Institution. Photo: Eugene Mantie. VIII. Courtesy of the Walter Hampden-Edwin Booth Theatre Collection and Library at The Players. Photo: Helga Photo Studio. IX. National Portrait Gallery, Smithsonian Institution. Photo: Eugene Mantie. X. National Portrait Gallery, Smithsonian Institution; lent by the National Gallery of Art. XI. Milwaukee Art Center. XII. Courtesy of Dorothy Stickney. Photo: Helga Photo Studio. XIII. Privately owned. Photo: courtesy of Hirschl and Adler Galleries. XIV. National Portrait Gallery, Smithsonian Institution. Photo: Eugene Mantie. XV. Ibid. XVI. Ibid. XVII. Courtesy of Regina Resnik and Arbit Blatas. XVIII. Courtesy of Kathryn Mostel. Photo: Eugene Mantie. XIX. The Art Institute of Chicago. XX. Art Gallery of Ontario, Toronto; gift of the Women's Committee Fund, 1966.

Index of Artists

Arabic numerals indicate figure numbers;
Roman numerals refer to color plates.

A

Adams, Wayman, 109
Agate, Frederick Styles, III

B

Barrymore, John, 85
Barthé, Richmond, 107, 110
Bedetti, A., 41
Biberman, Edward, 106, 121
Blatas, Arbit, 123, XVII
Bolasni, Saul, 103
Bouché, René, 114
Briggs, Henry Perronet, 26, VII

C

Caruso, Enrico, 3
Chaliapin, Boris, 67, 68, 113, 118
Chambers, Charles E., 69
Chase, William Merritt, 61
Christy, Howard Chandler, 62
Cifariello, Filippo, 65
Colin, M., 60
Currier, Nathaniel, 1, 2

D

Dali, Salvador, XIX
Dupont, Aime, 66
Durand, Asher B., 6, 7
Durang, John, 12, 13

E

Enters, Angna, 111

F

Falk, Benjamin J., 59
Falter, John, 90, XII
Finck, Furman, 105
Flagg, James Montgomery, 53, 83
Foote, John, 126
Fosburgh, James, 93

G

Genthe, Arnold, 74
Glackens, William, 80-81
Goldbeck, Walter Dean, 96
Gregory, Jack, 129

H

Haggin, Ben Ali, 101
Henri, Robert, 72, 95, XIII

Herter, Albert, 71
Hicks, Thomas, IX
Hirschfeld, Al, 119
Hoban, Russell, 128
Hoffman, Malvina, 82

I

Inman, Henry, 16, 18, 28, 31
Ivanowski, Sigismund de, 72

J

John, Augustus, XIV
Johnson, Eastman, 42

K

Kalman, Benjamin, 64
Kaulbach, Friedrich August von, 86, VI
Koerner, Henry, 122
Kuhn, Walt, 112

L

Larche, Raoul, 55
Longacre, James Barton, 4, 5
Luks, George, 54

M

Magnus, Eduard, 37
Meltsner, Paul, 90, XVI
Mostel, Zero, 120, XVIII
Mucha, Alphonse, 63

N

Neagle, John, 4-7, 14, 17, 23
Noguchi, Isamu, 9

O

Orpen, Sir William, 89

P

Peale, Charles Willson, 10, I

Pene du Bois, Guy, 92

R

Reyneau, Betsy Graves, 98
Rogers, John, 8, 38, 45-47
Rouland, Orlando, 52

S

Sargent, John Singer, 43, VIII
Schattenstein, Nikol, 91
Scott, William, 49
Simmons, Edward, 79
Sloan, John, 75, XI
Sloat, Rosemarie, 115, XV
Speicher, Eugene, 97
Spy. *See* Sir Leslie Ward
Sully, Thomas, 11, 15, 20, 27, II, IV, V

T

Toulouse-Lautrec, Henri, 57

V

Van Vechten, Carl, 102

W

Walkowitz, Abraham, 73
Ward, Sir Leslie, 39
Warhol, Andy, 127, XX
Wieczorek, Max, 70
Wiles, Irving R., 58, X